D1613110

C333875484

# 'I Wish I Had Your Wings'

# 'I Wish I Had Your Wings'

## A SPITFIRE PILOT AND OPERATION PEDESTAL, MALTA 1942

ANGUS MANSFIELD

First published 2016

The History Press
The Mill, Brimscombe Port
Stroud, Gloucestershire, GL5 2QG
www.thehistorypress.co.uk

British Library Cataloguing in Publication Data.
A catalogue record for this book is available from the British Library.

ISBN 978 0 7524 9782 2

Typesetting and origination by The History Press
Printed and bound in Great Britain by TJ International Ltd

# Contents

# Foreword

It is incredible how in times of danger, sincere and lasting friend-ships are formed. So it was with Johnnie and myself during the Battle of Malta. We flew daily in combat, often as a pair against the bombers and fighters attacking the island, and became firm and lasting friends.

Johnnie was a forceful character, pugnacious and fiery, with a wicked sense of humour which he retained even in the dark days of Malta. His laugh was infectious but he was not the sort to take rubbish from anybody. Always a pleasure to be with – his habit of twirling his moustache springs instantly to mind – it is a renewed pleasure for me to see him again in the pages of this book.

This book describes in detail the Malta convoys of 1942 and portrays graphically the bravery of the merchant seamen who were constantly attacked before reaching the island.

Allan Scott DFC

# Acknowledgements

My third book has taken several years of research and I am indebted to a great many people in helping me, but most of all to Sally Keyes, John Mejor's daughter and David Macfarlane's great-niece, who was brave enough to allow me to write her dad's and her great-uncle's story. I hope she feels that I have been able to tell it accurately and to do them both justice.

I have been able to use Johnnie's log books and papers, together with family papers from David Macfarlane that Sally was willing to share with me.

To anyone I have inadvertently omitted, I apologise in advance.

I have interviewed several pilots who flew with Johnnie Mejor and who were also in Malta at the time of Operation Pedestal.

Before his death, I had already been in touch with Jack Rae in New Zealand, who was able to recall his time on the island, having flown into Malta from the American aircraft carrier USS *Wasp* as part of the same Operation Calendar as Johnnie Mejor on 20 April 1942, and in turn gave me permission to use quotes from his own book *Kiwi Spitfire Ace*, published by Grub Street several years ago.

Geoffrey Wellum flew his Spitfire into Malta from HMS *Furious* as part of Operation Bellows and the wider Operation Pedestal on 11 August, just after HMS *Eagle* had been sunk. Having flown into Malta, he joined 1435 Squadron along with Johnnie Mejor. He is still alive and well and living in Cornwall, and gave me permission to use quotes from his book *First Light*, now a bestseller. Penguin Books were also good enough to give me permission to use the same.

Allan Scott first met Johnnie Mejor in Malta, they flew together with 1435 Squadron and were both posted back to the UK and joined the same Maintenance Unit at Colerne near Bath as test pilots, and, by a strange quirk of fate, the same 122 Squadron as part of the 2nd Tactical Air Force in the build-up to D-Day. They looked after each other in the air and on the ground and became the best of friends. Allan was best man when John and Cecile were married, is currently living in Shropshire and has written his own story, *Born to Survive*, published by Ellingham Press. He was also very willing to share his stories of their times together and give me permission to use quotes from his book, and has been good enough to write a foreword. When this book is published, he has agreed that he and I will play a game of golf and raise a glass to Johnnie. It will be my privilege, and all the more remarkable as Allan is now 94 and still plays.

The National Archives at Kew and the Caird Library at the National Maritime Museum in Greenwich both deserve a mention, as they willingly help anyone trying to research a project such as this.

The book would also not have been possible without the help of everyone at The History Press, but in particular Shaun Barrington and Jo De Vries.

Finally, a word of thanks to my wife, Sue, who has put up with my absence whilst I have researched and written this book. I could not do without her love and support.

# Prologue

# Early Morning
# 13 August 1942

*T*hey had made it through the night, but only just. Captain David Rattray Macfarlane OBE had manoeuvred his ship, the Melbourne Star, into position with what remained of the convoy in single line. Rochester Castle *was leading, followed by* Waimarama, *then his ship the* Melbourne Star *with the* Ohio *behind him.* Port Chalmers *was some way behind and had not caught up with them.*

*On the bridge of the* Melbourne Star, *Macfarlane peered into the darkness before first light and wondered what else could be thrown at the convoy. Only half the convoy had survived the night and daybreak would bring no relief, only more Axis bombers and, for all he knew, Italian cruisers and destroyers as well. Aboard the depleted escorts and merchant ships of the convoy, haggard and exhausted men stood ready to repel what could be the enemy's next decisive attack. Very few gave themselves much of a chance. Against everything that the Axis could launch against the remains of the convoy, there seemed little that the remaining ships could do except go down fighting.*

*Despite the repeated attacks, Macfarlane was aware that the damaged tanker the* Ohio *was still making decent progress. Supreme efforts were required to hold the damaged vessel on her course. Her deck had been split across the centre almost to her amidships and with every yaw of her helm the buckled metal tore and groaned, threatening to break the entire ship in half. It was necessary to keep a continuous 5 degrees on the starboard helm to compensate for the pull caused by the great gouge in her side. By 3 a.m. the tanker had managed to reach a speed of 13 knots and by dawn she had caught up with the remainder of the convoy.*

*They had been expecting attacks from the Italian Navy all night; it was a miracle that there had been none. In fact the Italians had withdrawn and steamed away from the convoy because Air Vice Marshal Park, in charge of the RAF on Malta, had sent out what available aircraft he had and ordered them to illuminate the Italian cruisers and regularly return to Malta, to convey to the Italians that a strike force of considerable size and power was on its way. This was followed up by an attack from a single Wellington and an 'illuminate and attack' call to non-existent Liberators, which resulted in the Italian cruisers making a course for Palermo.*

*Good fortune, fortitude and deception had all played their part, but this did not concern Rear Admiral Burrough, who had deployed what was left of his escorts to fight a defensive action against the expected surface attack from the Italians. The force available to him was hardly impressive, however. Other than three minesweeping destroyers, he could only muster a damaged cruiser, HMS* Kenya, *and HMS* Charybdis *as heavy ships and four big Tribal-class destroyers, including HMS* Pathfinder. *HMS* Bramham *was standing by the abandoned* Santa Elisa, *HMS* Penn *was coming up from astern with* Port Chalmers *while HMS* Ledbury *was close to the* Ohio, *but they were about 5 miles astern of the main body which now consisted of the* Melbourne Star, Waimarama *and* Rochester Castle.

## 1435 SQUADRON AIRBORNE

*Everything now depended on the convoy from the west. Johnnie Mejor squinted into the rising morning sun, wondering when they would receive the order to take off. Malta's surviving Beaufighters had patrolled what was left of the convoy in the hours of darkness as it slipped through the narrow channel between the coast of Tunis and the western tip of Sicily, but the really dangerous time began now, with the dawn, as the surviving merchant ships and oil tanker with their escorts entered 'bomb alley' and the final run to the beleaguered island.*

*The convoy was still hours away from the island, a nightmare journey through the most bitterly contested waters in the world, with the full weight of the* Luftwaffe *and* Regia Aeronautica *in southern Italy and Sicily intent on destroying what was left of it. Sometime during the morning, the convoy would reach a point 70 miles from Malta where relays of Spitfires from Takali and Hal Far – every available aircraft – could endeavour to provide a continual air umbrella over the ships. Before that point there was a 40-mile gap between first light and the maximum distance at which the Takali and Hal Far Spitfires could begin to provide cover. The Luqa Spitfires that had been fitted with long-range tanks would fill that gap. Only*

Luqa had a long enough strip of runway available to get the heavily laden fighters airborne.

Mejor looked at his watch. The squadron would be split into three sections of four aircraft and led by Wing Commander Pete 'Prosser' Hanks. Mejor felt a shiver run down his spine – he put it down to the aftermath of the 'Dog', an attack on the contents of his stomach from which he had only recently recovered. Mac – Ian Maclennan, a Canadian – had been right about the goat's milk after all, and Mejor still felt washed-out and in no fit state to fly a Spitfire into action against, possibly, twenty or thirty times their number. He felt shattered.

This morning, co-incidentally, Sykes and Tozer were his fitter and rigger, and Mejor was glad. He enjoyed the cheerful banter of the two airmen, even though he felt grim. At Luqa, in these hectic days of August 1942, it was rare to get the same ground crew twice; the pilots grabbed whatever fighter was serviceable and in the months that Mejor had been on the island, he had done the rounds of just about every blast pen around the perimeter. In his mind he went over the latest situation reports. The convoy was a long way behind schedule at the last report. Suddenly, he pushed himself away from the sandbags, startled by his airman's excited shout. The airman was pointing across the cratered airfield to G Shelter, where a Very flare had been fired and was tracing its smoky trail through the morning haze. Sykes, the fitter, was already in the Spitfire cockpit and by the time Mejor got there he had the engine running. The airman relinquished his place and helped Mejor to strap himself in, dropped off the wing as Mejor taxied forward and gave him a 'thumbs up' for good luck. The other Spitfires were also emerging from their blast pens, kicking up clouds of dust as they wove their way to the runway. Mejor kept his cockpit hood open for take-off and gained a few precious seconds of cooling fresh air.

The Spitfire rumbled forward, swaying slightly as he tried to line up with the centre of the runway and opened the throttle. The tail came up reluctantly as he eased the stick forward and the speed built up agonisingly slowly as the Merlin engine coped with the extra weight of the auxiliary fuel tank. It was the same, he recalled, all those months before, when he had taken off from the USS Wasp to fly to Malta. This time he had slightly more runway to play with but he was almost despairing that the fighter would ever leave the ground *when she bounced a couple of times and wallowed into the air, and the controls became more responsive as she steadily gained flying speed.*

*He pulled up the undercarriage and slammed the cockpit hood closed, turning the Spitfire quickly on the heading that ought to bring them close to the convoy, or what was left of it: 280 degrees magnetic. He formed up with the other Spitfires in formation. Radio silence was to be maintained until they were over the convoy or unless they got into trouble en route. There was no point advertising their presence or movements to the enemy. The squadron flew on steadily for several minutes. Over on the left, a lump of rock emerged from the sea, the island of Linosa. Beyond it was nothing but a vast expanse of the open Mediterranean. They had been airborne for nearly 30 minutes and by now should have been over the convoy. Mejor frowned and glanced at his cockpit instruments; there was nothing below him or the squadron, or anywhere in their vicinity as far as the eye could see. It occurred to him in a sudden, horrifying thought that perhaps they were too late, and that the convoy had already been wiped out.*

# 1

# John Mejor – Early Days

John Mejor was born in Antwerp on 12 July 1921, the son of a Belgian engineer and a Scottish mother. His father died when he was only 12 and his mother brought the family to Liverpool, where, pretty much penniless, she ran a sweet shop. John was educated at Bootle Grammar School, where he had a certain affinity with the Flemish headmaster, given his Belgian origins.

Emblazoned on the school badge of Bootle Grammar School was the motto of the town of Bootle: *Respice, Aspice, Prospice* (look to the past, look to the present, look to the future). We must remember the past: to learn from our mistakes, to take joy from our triumphs and to honour our origins. We must consider the present: to face daily challenges, to enjoy life without taking anything for granted and to be a good example for all. We must look to the future: to build a peaceful world for the next generation, to pass on our knowledge to our children and to be hopeful that tomorrow will always bring a brighter sunrise. The motto would stay with Mejor for the rest of his life.

Rather than go to university, Mejor enlisted in the RAF Volunteer Reserve at the age of 18 in the summer of 1940, at the height of the Battle of Britain, when there was such a shortage of pilots, and began his flying training at No. 22 Elementary Flying Training School (EFTS) Cambridge, completing it at No. 8 Service Flying Training School (SFTS) Montrose in Scotland.

Those passing simple examinations left for flying training. Some went to the United States or the Commonwealth, while the remainder were shared between Elementary Flying Training Schools, with No. 22 at Cambridge, using the Miles Magister and Tiger Moth trainers and a unit operated by Marshalls Ltd of Cambridge using civilian instructors in RAF uniform, where his aptitude for pilot training was assessed and considered suitable. They lived in requisitioned houses just outside the airfield, with very basic amenities and poor food. They did their day flying training at Bottisham airfield, about 5 miles east of Cambridge, sharing it with an Army co-operation unit of Tomahawks. Mejor had only been there a few days when he saw a Tomahawk do a flat spin that went in nose first. He was told the pilot lived but lost both his legs.

The course at Cambridge lasted about two months and formed the first of three parts of their flying training, which would take about six months in all, at the end of which, in theory, they would be ready to join an operational squadron. They were supposed to do a minimum of about 50 hours of flying in each element or at each training school, but flew in atrocious conditions much of the time. Low cloud, poor visibility and high winds were not unusual and gave him a good grounding.

He then reported to No. 8 Service Flying Training School at Montrose. Formed on 1 January 1936 at Montrose in No. 23 Group, it was transferred to No. 21 Group on 1 January 1939 and renamed No. 8 Service Flying Training School on 3 September that year. It was equipped with Harts and Oxfords for both single- and multi-engine training, but on 24 June 1940 it was re-classified as a single-engine (Group 1) school flying the Miles Master. All flying schools in existence prior to the start of the war were re-designated Service Flying Training Schools at the outbreak of war.

The Master was the newest of the RAF's advanced trainers, having been introduced shortly before the war. It was similar to the Hawker Hurricane in looks but not in performance. The Master was fitted with a Kestrel engine of some 75hp, so getting airborne was spectacular because of the kick from the extra power, and the aircraft swung due to the engine torque before it lifted into the air. Mejor quickly had to master the handling characteristics and technique required to get the best out of the aircraft. He practised straight and level flying, climbing, gliding, stalling – being wary of the sudden drop of the nose with the resultant loss of height, which was much more than he was used to – and then more practice, medium turns, take-off into wind, powered approaches and land-ings. It was the surge of power that he remembered.

The Wings examination proved straightforward and he was awarded his Wings on 9 July 1941.

A couple of weeks later, Mejor was posted to No. 7 Operational Training Unit at Hawarden, a few miles from Chester, where he would learn to fly Spitfires. Prior to the Second World War, air-crew completed their operational training on their squadrons, but once war had broken out and operations had begun, it became obvious that this could not be carried out by units and/or per-sonnel actively engaged on operations. At first, squadrons were removed from operations and were allocated the task of preparing new pilots and/or crews, but before long these training squadrons were re-designated Operational Training Units. Over the next month, Mejor concentrated on formation flying, dogfighting, aerobatics and circuits and bumps, together with firing his guns and practice interceptions. By 10 November he had completed the final leg of his training at No. 57 OTU and his course was finished. Assessed as average, he was posted to the newly forming 132 Squadron at Peterhead on the North Sea coast of Scotland, 30 miles north of Aberdeen. Initially they were equipped with Mk I Spitfires but soon moved up to the Mk II, and by early 1942 to the Mk V. The 132 Squadron was a cosmopolitan squadron, with Mejor from Belgium, a couple of Canadians – Bill MacRae and Wally McLeod – and Free French, Polish and one Czech pilot, as well as a Rhodesian and of course a few British, includ-ing the flight commanders and their new squadron leader, Alfie W. Bayne DFC.

All the Canadians were eventually posted out, and the Free French and Polish pilots (with whom Mejor had a particular affinity, given his Flemish background) became part of their own national squadrons. For the eight months he was with 132 Squadron, it never left Scotland and not a single gun was fired in anger. The only time they saw an aircraft with black crosses was one day in November when a Junkers Ju 88 popped out of low cloud, dropped a string of bombs on the camp, killed one pilot on the ground with machine-gun fire and escaped into cloud without being detected by radar, leaving them questioning the reliability of their low-level radar. It was guarding against this kind of hit-and-run attack that had them frequently scrambled, in pairs during the day and singly at night, to intercept anything approaching from the east without a functioning IFF (Identification, Friend or Foe), the early transponder. Everything they intercepted turned out to be friendlies, all with their IFF off. They were a mixed bag, from Whitleys to, on one occasion, an early B17 in RAF markings.

No. 132 Squadron, winter 1942. (J.G. Mejor)

Pilot officers Arthur Russell, John Mejor and Bugs Burgess, 132 Squadron, 1942. (J.G. Mejor)

Hit-and-run raids usually took advantage of low cloud cover, ideal for the Germans but not for the RAF. It has been said that Scotland is second only to the Aleutian Islands for bad flying weather, at least in winter, and the locals claimed that this was the worst winter in living memory. When the runways were not snowed in, it was routine to be scrambled into ceilings as low as 300ft. With no navigational radio, they depended on radar to vector them back down out of cloud, preferably over the sea. From there they were on their own. None of them had had any previous actual instrument time, only dual under the hood, and none in Spitfires. They were ill-prepared to quickly become virtual all-weather interceptors and paid the price. In a very short time at least six pilots were killed, about 25 per cent of the squadron. Two spun in out of cloud; two collided in cloud; one missed the field and hit the mountains not far to the west. Another, on a night scramble, failed to acknowledge repeated orders to return to base and was last seen leaving the radar screen in the direction of Norway, which he had insufficient fuel to reach.

There were also lighter moments. Many RAF fields were designed like an overturned saucer, probably to improve drainage, so that on landing the Spitfire always ended up going downhill. At low speed, the Spitfire's rudder was ineffective and without a steerable tail wheel, differential braking was needed to steer. Loss of brakes could mean trouble. One night Bill MacRae landed a bit long, probably overused the brakes to slow down, and they faded. He switched off and sat helpless as the Spitfire slowly rolled downhill, veering toward the side of the runway. First one wheel dropped off into the mud, swinging the machine around, so the second wheel followed. The tail rose high but dropped back before the propellor could hit the ground. He was lucky, but several others were not. Paul, one of three Free French pilots they had, lost his brakes one night and ran off the end of the runway. When they got to him, his aircraft was balanced, vertically, with the spinner and propellor imbedded in the mud. Paul was looking down at the ground from his lofty perch, repeating over and over 'sheet, sheet', to everyone's great amusement.

The boredom and monotony of operations in the middle of winter in Scotland led Mejor to answer a call for volunteers for a special operation involving 'hazardous service', with no idea of what it would be. He boarded a train to Glasgow, then to Greenock, from where a van transported him to a well-guarded wharf, whereupon he set eyes on the huge form that he later learnt to be the American aircraft carrier USS *Wasp*. This massive ship was there courtesy of President Roosevelt, being his answer to Winston Churchill's urgent plea for help with the transport of Spitfires so desperately needed for the defence of Malta. Malta would be Mejor's next stop.

# 2

# David Rattray Macfarlane: Early Days and First Convoy to Malta, Operation Substance, 1941

D avid Macfarlane was born in Auckland, New Zealand, in 1895 and first went to sea as a 15-year-old with the Union Steam Ship Company in 1910.

He joined the Blue Star Line in August 1915 as third officer of the *Brodstane* and was promoted to second officer on the same ship before joining the steamer *Brodmede* as second officer in 1917. He was on board when the ship was torpedoed and shelled by a German submarine in September 1917, but she was able to make her escape and reach Gibraltar safely.

The Blue Star Line had been formally registered in 1911 and the first ships were registered with Lloyds Register of Shipping between 1912 and 1913. Prior to the First World War, seven refrigerated ships sailed under the Blue Star Line banner, carrying eggs and other perishables to England from China. By the First World War it had twelve vessels, all their names starting with 'Brod' after Evelene Brodstone, who later married William Vestey. A considerable profit was made over these years with the carriage of beef to supply the Allied armies in France and it was for these services that William Vestey was honoured by becoming a baron.

Between the wars, Macfarlane served on several of the Blue Star Line vessels, including his first command as captain of the *Celtic Star*, and while peacetime brought a slow-down in promotion, his undoubted ability and winning personality still ensured his promotion to master by the time he had reached his early 30s. The Blue Star line ships were amongst the fastest of their time.

Lorraine Vines, a passenger aboard the *Imperial Star* on a journey from Australia to England before the Second World War, recalled her journey on board the ship:

The Imperial Star was one of the newest of the Blue Star Line fleet, she had a good turn of speed and with favourable conditions covered nearly 420 nautical miles in a day. Because of her speed, she had to seek the cover of darkness when overtaking a Royal

Mail passenger liner; it was considered 'infra dig' for a cargo vessel to travel faster than His Majesty's mail. Her Captain was David Macfarlane, who was later to become a much-decorated Merchant Navy Commander following the famous convoys to Malta. We occupied two double cabins, each with a bathroom. Our baths were of salt water but each day our steward would bring us large jugs of warm water to help wash off the salt. The fare to London was £60 per person or £110 return. There were twelve passengers, who were pleasant if not memorable. We sat at the Captain's table. On the second day out of Sydney, Captain Mac took Judith and me on a tour of the ship, first of all for'ard where we could lean over and watch the beautiful bow wave made by her clean-cut lines. From there he took us aft to have a good look at her length. I expressed a fear that I might not make a good sailor. Captain Mac explained that was why he [had] taken us to the extremes of the ship, where we would experience the most motion; having passed this test without a qualm, he said we should have no worries. Being almost fully laden with cargo, we were fairly low in the water so our only movement was that of pitching, a much more comfortable feeling than a roll.

By the outbreak of war in 1939, Macfarlane was still in command of the *Imperial Star* and had an early introduction to the perils of conflict when, on the homeward leg of his voyage from Australia and approaching Britain, a surfaced U-boat attacked. The *Imperial Star* was armed with a 6in gun aft, a heavier weapon than that carried by the German submarine, and the Germans broke off the engagement and submerged, only to resurface and resume the engagement. Thanks to her superior speed and skilful seamanship under Macfarlane, the *Imperial Star* was able to make good her escape.

His next voyage was in command of the *Auckland Star*, which had been fitted out at Belfast when the war began. With the surrender of France at the end of June 1940, the German Navy – *Kriegsmarine* – acquired the use of strategically important west coast French ports and had soon established several U-boat bases along the Bay of Biscay. The northern bases of Brest, Lorient and Saint Nazaire were ideally situated for attacks on shipping using the south-west approaches to Britain and Ireland. Again sailing alone and on the homeward journey from Australia to Britain, the *Auckland Star* sailed from Townsville, Queensland, in May 1940 and called at Sydney, Cape Town and Cape Verde. She had reached a position 90 miles south-west of Ireland early in the morning of July 28 1940. As she had no escort, she had been steaming at her full speed of 16.5 knots and 'zig-zagging' when she was torpedoed on the port side between No. 5 and No. 6 holds. Chief Officer Farnell had just entered the wheelhouse when the first torpedo hit. He was adjusting his night vision when an almighty crack and a violent shudder shattered the solitude of the morning. Captain Macfarlane soon joined his chief officer on the bridge as he gave orders to stop engines. The *Auckland Star* started to settle at once and, unable to control the flooding and with the ship well down in the water aft, Captain Macfarlane was reluctantly forced to give orders to abandon ship some 30 minutes after being struck by the first torpedo, telling his officers to stand by until she sank. Not content with seeing the ship go down, the impatient U-boat commander, Otto Kretschemer, in *U-99* torpedoed her again, this strike hitting the engine room, hurling debris high into the air, followed by a third torpedo when she was still afloat some 75 minutes after the first blow, hitting the ship close to No. 2 hatch. About a quarter of an hour later, at about 5.30 a.m., the *Auckland Star* rolled over to port, threw her bow in the air and sank by the stern, taking with her the large cargo of nearly 10,700 tons of refrigerated meat and general cargo, including lead, steel, hides, wheat and other refrigerated products. A distress signal had been sent out.

Left behind were four lifeboats with the entire complement of the crew of the *Auckland Star*. Although a little cramped, the lifeboats were well provisioned and well founded. The Irish coast was only a short distance away and the weather was favourable.

Able Seaman J.M. O'Driscoll takes up the story in his log book:

**28/07/1940**

Clock advanced 11 minutes, it was a fine night. Torpedoed 3.10 a.m. port quarter. Felt a terrific thud and shudder and saw a blinding flash. Collected a few odds and ends and took to boats 3.20 a.m. Second torpedo sent amidships just as we were pulling away at 4 a.m. approx. Port plates were flying in the air and streams of water also. Third torpedo sent amidships at about 4.15 a.m. Submarine surfaced about 5 minutes afterwards to watch the gallant *Auckland Star* heel gracefully over on her port side and the bow rise in the air and then down by 4.45 a.m. Sub moved off. SOS answered by Land's End almost immediately – we are 64 miles off south-west coast of Ireland. Sails put up 5.15 a.m. We were last boat to leave. Captain Macfarlane came in our boat but transferred to no. 1 boat just afterwards. He looked all in. Everybody acted just as if they were changing watches! Captain was cool as a cucumber, magnificent. The only injury was a cut cheek to greaser Joe Blain, one of the poop lookouts. A Sunderland flying boat appeared 7.55 a.m. and circled round until 9.30 a.m. Biscuits and brandy once or twice during morning, dinner at 1 p.m. was corned beef and biscuits with water.

Another flying boat circled round us at 2 p.m. – plane landed at 2.20 p.m. Rowed like hell towards her, sails up as well! Pilot made for Captain's boat and away again by 2.35 p.m. A destroyer is supposed to be coming out this evening. An Irish Coaster passed us at 4 p.m. but did not take any notice of us! Baling out while rowing. Tins of milk and biscuits passed around. Brandy again too, three of the four boats still together [at] 1.50 a.m.

**29/07/1940**

Slept on oars placed fore and aft. Not a bad bed when you are tired but rather cold. Baling out at 3 a.m. and brandy passed around. I had a good swig. We are going to make our own way in. Fine morning again. We have now been in the boats 24 hours and it is 25 hours since we caught the unlikely blow. Still, thank god for our lives. Still wise-cracking – 'I think we will have ham and eggs or a steak, and what no tea?'! All in good spirits. Instead we get biscuits, bully beef, skimmed milk and water. My atlas is being used by Captain and his mate – good old sixpenny atlas. Sighted land about 1 p.m. and changed course.

**30/07/1940**

Been rowing nearly all night, land coming slowly nearer. Flares used but no success. Time now 5.30 a.m. and 50 hours in boats. No sign of the 1st Mate's boat since 1 p.m. yesterday. At 8 a.m. little skin fishing boats off the Blasket Islands came out to see if they could assist. Captain asked them to get a motor boat to tow us in. At 9.50 a.m. a fishing motor boat D.167 came to us – at last! First Mate's boat has not turned up yet. Passed kettle of tea and bread from boat to boat. Landed Dingle 12.45 a.m. Whole town turned out on wharf. Marched through streets – with flags given to us by people – towards the police barracks. Taken in back entrance of pub – drinks given. Fifty-seven hours in boats. Went to church and gave my thanks to almighty god and then went to the presbytery and asked the priest to hear confession, which he did. Gave up brandy and tobacco. I got my atlas back from the Captain and fitted out with complete outfits, free cigarettes and drinks, meals and bed. Absolute freedom of the town and really good-hearted people. I hope advantage is not taken of them. Understand mate's boat picked up late afternoon off Clifton Galway 80 miles up the coast. Roll call at the barracks and return of identity cards.

**31/07/1940**

Not had a cigarette this morning – free drinks at Murphy's. Went to Guard House and put my belongings in a sack. Report to barracks at 12 a.m. and special buses for us. Captain given a rousing cheer and 'for he's a jolly good fellow'. Left Dingle 12.30 a.m. and caught 2 p.m. train to Dublin.

Not one man was lost from the *Auckland Star* sinking and it is clear that his crew held Captain Macfarlane in the highest regard.

A year later Macfarlane was put in command of the MV *Melbourne Star* and made Commodore of the six merchant ships that would try and get through to the besieged island of Malta as part of Operation Substance. The idea for the convoy was to take advantage of the German's preoccupation with the new front opened in Russia. This meant they had also redeployed squadrons of the *Luftwaffe* from Sicily and Sardinia and in doing so had provided Malta with a temporary lull. The need to run a convoy to Malta was self-evident. In particular, Malta's stocks of food were depleted and the campaigns in Greece and Crete had drained naval resources. Anti-aircraft shells and aviation fuel were nearly exhausted and in dire need of replenishment. The redeployment of some *Luftwaffe* squadrons still left the Italians, who had about 200 high level bombers and some Junkers, who still posed a serious threat to shipping. There was also the Italian Navy, which posed a greater threat. By June 1941 the Italians had available to them five battleships, ten cruisers, twenty destroyers and thirty to forty MAS boats or E-boats, plus numerous submarines.

For the July convoy the Admiralty summoned six merchantmen – the *Melbourne Star* (10,800 tons), *City of Pretoria* (7,900 tons), *Sydney Star* (11,000 tons), *Durham* (10,900 tons), *Deucalion* (7,800 tons) and *Port Chalmers* (8,500 tons) – and a troopship, the *Leinster* (4,300 tons). The escort for the first part of the convoy consisted of the battlecruiser *Renown*, battleship *Nelson*, aircraft carrier *Ark Royal*, cruisers *Edinburgh*, *Manchester*, *Arethusa* and *Hermoine*, with a cruiser minelayer *Manxman* and seventeen further destroyers. Vice Admiral Sir James Sommerville was in command.

It was clear that something special was happening, even at the embarkation stage. In Swansea the Blue Star Line *Deucalion* began to take on stores. Engineer S.J. Dodd recalled:

> It was sensed that this was a special voyage because we [were] loading general food supplies and *Deucalion* had limited but useful refrigeration cargo space, a lot of War Department equipment, loads of bully beef and endless drums of high octane aviation fuel. The special voyage feeling was confirmed when a contingent of soldiers embarked. They had pretty basic accommodation and carried all their own gear but were made as comfortable as possible. I learned later they were crack AA [anti-aircraft] gunners from the Cheshire regiment. *Deucalion* joined the convoy and headed south.

On board *Sydney Star*, six gunners and an NCO had been taken on board. A. Cockburn remembered:

> We had been issued with naval clothes, lifebelts, tropical dress and civilian clothes. I was comforted when the *Sydney Star* broke out into the Atlantic with the rest of the convoy and found we were in the company of the *Ark Royal*, a number of heavy cruisers and destroyer. Quite soon the *City of Pretoria* and *Port Chalmers* joined up.

Vice Admiral Sommerville sent a message to all ships via a destroyer to each master of the merchant ships. Macfarlane recalled, 'The force was still 150 miles from Gibraltar and the message was shot by rocket line and was the Admiral's own personal message.' It read:

For over twelve months Malta has resisted all attacks of the enemy. The gallantry displayed by the garrison and people of Malta has aroused admiration throughout the world. To enable their defence to be continued, it is essential that your ships with their valuable cargoes, should arrive safely in Grand Harbour. The Royal Navy will escort and assist you in this great mission, you on your part can assist the Royal Navy by giving strict attention to the following points. Don't make smoke. Don't show any lights at night. Keep good station. Don't straggle. If your ship is damaged keep her going at the best possible speed. Provided every officer and man realises it is up to him to do his duty to the very best of his ability, I feel sure we shall succeed. Remember that the watchword is *the convoy must get through*.

The convoy approached Gibraltar in dense fog, so much so that they could not see the Rock. There were also other problems. The troop ship *Pasteur* had failed to join the convoy and *Leinster* had run aground. Despite all the planning and the sizeable escorts, there were losses. When Force H neared the narrows, its major units turned around to return to Gibraltar. This the usual practice so that the ships were not put to an unacceptable level of risk, but it left the convoy with only cruisers and destroyers to provide protection. The first casualty was the *Manchester*. On 23 July two Italian MAS boats launched torpedoes at the cruiser, then at around 9.30 a.m. nine Italian bombers attacked. *Nelson* still provided distant cover and, with the rest of the protection ships, opened fire.

Stan Dodd on board *Deucalion* recalled, 'It rained down with bombs, the *Ark Royal* seemed to be their chief target. We watched bombs dropping all around her but she was not hit, probably due to expert navigation and steady AA fire.' During a pause in the attack the *Manchester* was hit by either a torpedo or a bomb, which severely damaged the cruiser. Chief Petty Officer Hughes said, 'Poor old *Manchester* was hit in an oil fuel tank. Adjacent compartments were flooded and two of her engines were put out of action, but we learned later that they managed to get her back to Gibraltar.' Twenty-six men were killed on board *Manchester* and she was escorted back to Gibraltar for repairs by four destroyers. CPO Hughes also recalled that the soldiers aboard were a great help in backing up the crew in damage control and dragging survivors from the wreckage, so much so that Captain Drew broadcast a tribute to the ship's company and the soldiers on board, 'Your courage and wonderful behaviour has saved our ship.'

Almost immediately the destroyer *Fearless* was also struck by a torpedo, which disabled her. She was taken in tow but was unable to be saved and the *Forester*, her sister ship, had to sink her. Stan Dodd recalls further:

> We could hear MAS boats in the pitch dark roaring through the shipping lanes and aircraft above. Frequently the destroyers exposed their searchlights and they let go with all they had – all was acrid smoke, brilliant blue and orange as the big guns were fired, and then a few seconds of dark and quiet until the next time. All this went on for quite a few hours. It was too exciting to be frightening.

During one of these last skirmishes and in the early morning of 24 July the convoy remained in two columns and was about 4 miles east of Pantelleria when one of the MAS boats attacked the *Sydney Star*, which was torpedoed and damaged on the port side of No. 3 hold. Heavily listing to port, for safety's sake Captain Horn decided to transfer the 464 troops he had aboard to another ship. Most of them were from the 32nd Light Anti-Aircraft (AA) Regiment. It was still dark but luckily the sea was calm and the weather fine. The destroyer *Nestor* closed in and the transfer of the troops started with three lifeboats, but was painfully slow. Being so close to the island of Pantelleria and with dawn approaching, Captain Horn asked

*Nestor* to come alongside, which she did and all the troops were successfully transferred, together with some of the crew. Captain Horn and other essential crew remained on board.

The holds were sealed and, although No. 3 hold had around 33ft of water and the adjacent Nos 1 and 2 each about 6ft, the engine room remained dry. Captain Horn recalled, 'I therefore informed the Commander of the destroyer that I would make an attempt to reach our destination, some 130 miles off, under our own power.' The *Nestor* remained as close escort. As dawn broke fine and clear, with a light haze, three attacks by small groups of torpedo bombers were beaten off by the guns on the *Sydney Star* and *Nestor*. There was then a brief respite until 9.30 a.m. when there were more high-altitude air attacks. Horn recalled, 'Helm manoeuvred to best advantage in evading the bombs and attack repulsed by ship's guns. One enemy plane was hit and seen to lose height with black smoke pouring from its tail.'

The *Sydney Star* was down by the head and too big a target to be left alone, and at 10.30 a.m. she was subjected to a further high level attack. Her speed was increased but the flooded ship listed heavily as full helm was used for twisting and turning to avoid the attacks.One bomb narrowly missed, showering the ship with fragments and water, so close was its burst. The water was gaining so much in Nos 1, 2 and 3 holds that when she heeled over to the helm the water rushed over to the low side and held her there, increasing the list.

By now, Horn said, 'We were about 15 miles from Malta so reduced speed to 10 knots as a precaution and then to 5 knots to prevent the bulkheads collapsing.' They finally entered the swept channel through the minefields off Malta at around 1.45 p.m., picking up a pilot to take her in about half an hour later. With three tugs grappling to get her under any sort of control, she was finally berthed around 4 p.m. She still had a heavy list to starboard and was 12ft down by the bow, drawing 42ft forward and 29ft aft.

Divers reported that the hole caused by the torpedo was approximately 40ft by 16ft and it was a miracle that she had stayed afloat.

In fact all the merchant ships of the convoy reached Malta with their valuable cargoes and Captain Macfarlane and Captain Horn were both awarded the OBE for their outstanding services.

Vice Admiral J.F. Somerville, commander of Operation Substance, commented in his report:

> That the operation was successfully carried out is due in no small measure to the behaviour of the merchant ships in convoy. Their manoeuvring and general conduct was excellent and caused me no anxiety whatever. I had complete confidence that orders given to them by me would be understood and promptly carried out. Their steadfast and resolute behaviour during air and E-boat attacks was most impressive and encouraging to us all. Particular credit is due to [the] Captain of the SS *Melbourne Star*, Commodore of the convoy, who set a high standard and never failed to appreciate directly what he should do. SS *Durham* experienced piston trouble in her port engine and it was evident that her engines required careful nursing. Nevertheless, she was able to maintain a speed of 14 knots throughout the critical period on Day 3 and Day 4, which was only one knot less than her accredited maximum speed.

Captain Macfarlane's OBE was listed in the *London Gazette* in December 1941:

> To be Additional Officers of the Civil Division of the Most Excellent Order of the British Empire – Captain David Rattray Macfarlane, Master. Captain Macfarlane was Commodore of an important convoy. By his steadfast and resolute behaviour during enemy attacks he set a high standard and it is largely due to his leadership that the Operation was successful.

3

# Malta and the
# Struggle for Survival

For the Italians and Germans, Malta was both a natural and vital target. Lying within 60 to 65 miles of the large Italian air bases in Sicily, the island dominated the key strategic centre of the Mediterranean. While Malta remained in British hands the Royal Navy could fight its way through the Mediterranean; but if Malta were to fall into enemy hands, the consequences would be unthinkable. Not only would the Mediterranean route be closed to British shipping, but there would be no staging base for aircraft and troop movements to North Africa.

In March 1942 Air Vice Marshal Lloyd's request to have Spitfires sent to Malta was granted and on 7 March the first Spitfires bound for Malta took off from HMS *Eagle* near Gibraltar. Whilst they rallied the morale of the beleaguered island, there were not enough of them to make a critical difference and they remained hopelessly outnumbered. What was needed was more Spitfires and more supplies.

The Governor of Malta, General Dobbie, remained concerned at what might happen if further supplies did not get through. Wheat, flour, fodder, oil, coal and ammunition were all urgently needed. As flour was in such short supply, bread could not be made, and although hot meals were served by the 'victory kitchens' each day, starvation and hunger were rife. Against this backdrop the bombing continued to be indiscriminate and wrecked houses, blocked roads and blew water mains. Many Maltese civilians were living almost permanently in the underground shelters or catacombs and it had now become a battle of existence. The deficiency in the diet began to lead to disease and the Governor warned that for all its resolve, the population of Malta was gradually starving and the island might fall. Dobbie was shortly to be replaced by Lord Gort VC, the decision being taken by Churchill and·the War Cabinet who felt that Dobbie needed a rest.

A few days later King George VI conferred the award of the George Cross on the garrison and people of Malta. The award could not have been made at a more grim moment and it was taken as a symbol of the King's trust in the will of the island to resist and endure what was in store for them. The aerodromes and Grand Harbour continued to be bombed, but the bombing was indiscriminate – many thousands of buildings were hit in Valletta and the surrounding towns, and over 300 civilians were killed. On the airfields, where there was work to be constantly done, the attacks indicated when it was time to go to the shelters; nevertheless, the civilians spent most of the time in and out of the shelters. A vast number slept underground. Gas, water and electrical services continued to be hit and Valletta had to endure constant attacks without any of these services for almost five months. Hot meals and drinks became more infrequent. Water reservoirs had been destroyed and there was so little oil that none could be spared for the pumps to draw water from the underground stores, so there was little for drinking or sanitation. Food and above all sleep were in short supply. In the towns there were tons of rock blocking streets and dozens of unexploded bombs to hamper movements and clearance. It was often a scene of complete and utter devastation, and a harsh and frightening existence.

The situation in Malta remained critical, with the population starving and the threat of invasion hanging over them. Churchill was insistent that more Spitfires needed to be sent; the question remained how to get them there. Of the aircraft carriers, HMS *Argus* was not available and HMS *Eagle* was being repaired and likely to be out of action for almost a month. Extremely urgent action was needed. Churchill appealed to the president of the United States, Roosevelt, asking whether their huge aircraft carrier USS *Wasp* might be available to transport urgently required Spitfires through the Straits of Gibraltar, allowing them to fly off within range of Malta.

He had cabled Roosevelt on 1 April:

1. Air attacks on Malta are very heavy. There are now in Sicily about 400 German and 200 Italian fighters and bombers. Malta can now muster only 20 or 30 serviceable fighters. We keep feeding Malta with Spitfires in packets of 16 loosed from HMS *Eagle* from about 600 miles west of Malta. This has worked a good many times quite well, but HMS *Eagle* is now laid up for a month by defects in her steering gear. There are no Spitfires in Egypt. HMS *Argus* is too small and too slow, and moreover she has to provide fighter cover for the carrier launching the Spitfires and for the escorting force. We would use HMS *Victorious*, but unfortunately the lifts are too small for the Spitfires. Therefore there will be a whole month without any Spitfire reinforcements.

2. It seems likely, from extraordinary enemy concentration on Malta, that they hope to exterminate our air defence in time to reinforce either Libya or their Russian offensive. This would mean that Malta would be at the best powerless to interfere with reinforcements and supplies to Rommel and our chances of resuming the offensive against him at an early date ruined.

3. Would you be willing to allow your carrier *Wasp* to do one of these trips, provided details are satisfactorily agreed between the Navy staff? With her broad lifts, capacity and length, we estimate that *Wasp* could take 50 or more Spitfires. Unless it were necessary for her to fuel, *Wasp* could proceed through the Straits of Gibraltar without calling at Gibraltar until the return journey, as the Spitfires would be embarked in the Clyde.

4. Thus instead of not being able to give Malta any further Spitfires during April, a powerful Spitfire force could be flown into Malta at a stroke and give us a chance of inflicting a very severe and possibly

decisive check on the enemy. Operations might take place during the third week of April.

Roosevelt agreed and so the USS *Wasp* was made ready at Glasgow to receive the Spitfires and volunteer pilots from 601 County of London Squadron and 603 City of Edinburgh Squadron.

Every pilot on arrival, including John Mejor, was stunned by the scale of the operation on board the *Wasp* and the spirit of Anglo–American co-operation. The Mk Vc Spitfires, which had four cannon, were being efficiently lifted by crane onto the carrier's flight deck while all around them the rest of the required spares and materials also flowed on board. The Spitfires were painted a pale blue camouflage, slightly lighter in shade to the one Mejor had been used to on operations with 132 Squadron in the UK, but a reminder they were going to a different theatre of war.

Mejor's first experience on board was to be warmly welcomed with a real southern US accent. His sole personal possessions were in a kit bag that weighed little more than 10lb, as they all had instructions to take very little in view of the maximum flying weight of the Spitfires. After being shown to a comfortable-looking bunkroom, he was offered a tour of the vast ship, which proved an expedition in itself. The entire ship gave off an order of spick and span orderliness. Everything gleamed, lamp glasses glinted and all equipment was stowed ready for use. The whole impression was one of maximum efficiency against a background of constant activity, and on the flight deck he was able to watch the Spitfires being loaded by crane, pushed into a giant lift and then taken down to the large hangar deck.

The *Wasp* left Glasgow on 13 April carrying forty-seven Spitfires for Malta, escorted by HMS *Renown* and six destroyers. Mejor and many of the pilots were surprised to learn that the American ship was teetotal, but cola and fruit drinks were plentiful in supply. Officers were accommodated two to a cabin, most had air-conditioning and there were any amount of American magazines available. Aircraft occupied the hangar floor and were lashed to the ceiling. The Spitfires' wheels were steadied by wood blocks, their wing tips lashed to the deck by ropes and cables, and more were suspended from the roof girders, slung there by canvas loops which swayed gently as the big aircraft carrier rolled.

Mejor still did not know where he was being posted but all the pilots were briefed by Wing Commander Maclean, a New Zealander. He told them that they were to be taken into the Mediterranean, just north of Algiers, and there, out of range of the *Luftwaffe*, the Spitfires would be flown off the flight deck to Malta, keeping close to the African coast. This information had barely registered with Mejor and the other pilots when they were also told they would have 90-gallon auxiliary tanks under their fuselages, which they must switch over to immediately after take-off. If for some reason the switchover failed, they would have nowhere to go. This prospect did not fill Mejor with joy! Attempting a landing back on the carrier was not recommended. For a start, he had had no training in taking off from the carrier, let alone landing back on her. In any event, the Spitfires were not fitted with arrester gear – the large tail hook which carrier-based fighters used to pick up the arrester wire that stopped them from running off the flight deck.

Assuming the switchover worked as planned, he would have enough fuel to get to Malta but with very little spare. With the extra 90 gallons of fuel in the drop tanks, the Spitfire V still had a range of between 950 miles – if the tank was carried to the destination – or 1,050 miles if the tank was dropped when empty. Since the distance to fly to Malta would be approximately 660 miles, it left a fair margin in case of unexpected headwinds or they had to fight their way through to reach the island. The extra tank and the 90 gallons of fuel together weighed about 770lbs and this meant that the Spitfires would be taking off already overloaded. There would be little margin for safety and no unnecessary weight could be carried. Two of the four cannons were left unloaded and only 60 rounds were loaded in each of the other two. Mejor wondered what on earth he had let himself in for – an out of the frying pan into the fire choice!

It would be the largest reinforcement of Spitfires to be flown to Malta. None of them were sure what to expect and it resulted in a certain amount of panic buying from the ship's stores, which were fortunately well stocked. In order to get into the Mediterranean without being seen by enemy agents on the shores of Spain or North Africa, the fleet was going to have to run through the Straits of Gibraltar in the dead of night.

On 19 April they passed through the Straits and met up with two further cruisers and destroyers to bolster the escort. They were taking no chances; the Spitfires had to get through. It was planned that they would take off the following morning in four groups, led by Squadron Leader 'Jumbo' Gracie, who had been in Malta already but had returned to England to argue the case for more reinforcements. The US Navy Air Commander instructed them on procedures for take-off. During the launching operation the carrier would be committed to sailing a straight course in broad daylight within easy reach of enemy airfields, so the sooner the pilots were away after the launch had begun, the shorter the time the USS *Wasp* would be exposed to enemy attack. Later that afternoon the first twelve Spitfires would be taken up on the flight deck and arranged aft to leave room in the hangar to lower the aircraft suspended from the ceiling. At first light the following morning, the carrier would turn into the wind and its own squadron of Martlet fighters would take off to provide air cover for the Spitfires as they took off. As the last aircraft began its take-off run, the Spitfire in the hangar nearest the lift would start its engine, and the lift would then go down to pick it up and take it to the flight deck. The pilot would need to taxi forwards so that the lift could go down for the next Spitfire, which had in the meantime also started its engine. The whole operation would be complicated and the pilot instructions were minute and detailed. Above all else, they had to follow the deck crew instructions implicitly.

Mejor and the other pilots were briefed again on the take-off from the carrier, an exercise in itself as none of them had been trained for such an event. The technique was to rev up to 3,000rpm on the brakes, then release the brakes and select emergency boost override. After take-off the Spitfires were to form up in four formations, each formation departing when ready. After leaving the *Wasp* they were to fly along the north coast of Algeria and Tunisia as far as Cap Bon, then south-east to go around the enemy-held island of Pantelleria before heading due east for Malta. The pilots of the reinforcement force received a further briefing for their take-off the following morning from their US Navy Air Commander. They would get weather reports from Malta and would not be launched unless clear skies were forecast over their entire route. This would be important because the only navigational equipment they would carry would be maps, compasses and watches. For the final part of the journey they would get radar bearings from Malta.

Dawn on 20 April was the planned take-off time. Twelve Spitfires had been moved up onto the flight deck. At 4.15 a.m. John was up and having breakfast with the rest of the pilots, aware that there had been a major problem overnight. Up until the night before, the fuel tanks for the Spitfires had been kept empty for safety reasons. However, now that they were being fitted some of the auxiliary tanks had developed leaks. In spite of the very real hazards, the crew of the *Wasp* had managed to repair them overnight – a remarkable feat. Each of the pilots went to their allocated Spitfires on the hangar deck, and one by one were pushed backwards towards the lift, then up onto the flight deck and moved off the lift for the next Spitfire, and so on. Aircraft engines then had to be started. Mejor had been warned that if an aircraft engine didn't start or showed any problem, then it was likely the Spitfire would be pushed over the side as time was critical. The *Wasp*'s own Martlet fighters were circling above to offer protection in the take-off phase.

Luckily Mejor's engine did start without a problem. Minimum time was taken to bring the temperature up to safety, then a quick cockpit check – and it had to be quick – and he was guided into take-off position. The captain of the *Wasp*, true to his word, had the ship at maximum knots into a welcome headwind. Sat there, with brakes hard on, the rev-up signal was given and he opened the throttle steadily until he could feel the tailplane trying to rise and the Spitfire straining to go. Mejor knew the drill by heart, snapped the brakes off, gained speed rapidly, the deck suddenly disappeared and then he was up and airborne before he knew it. Once he had gained a little height and formed up with twelve more from 603 Squadron in loose formation, he switched to the fuel in the drop tank and was relieved to see the engine continue to run – at least the drop tank feed worked – and turned due east for Malta. When they reached their cruising altitude of 10,000ft they throttled back to 2,050rpm to get the most out of each gallon of fuel. At first the skies were clear of cloud and, to the south of them, Mejor could make out the reddish brown of the mountains that ran along the Algerian coast. As he settled down for the long flight, and before boredom set in, he remembered he was worried about losing concentration in case they came under attack. However, the flight proved largely uneventful. By the time they passed over Pantelleria, they did see some Messerschmitt Me 109s but no contact was made:

**20 April 1942**
Log Book: Spitfire Vb – Aircraft Carrier *Wasp* – Malta along north coast of Africa, sighted Me 109s over Pantelleria

After Pantelleria the skies cleared up completely and Mejor's first sight of Malta was the cloud of dust towering over the island from

No. 603 Squadron pilots on the deck of USS *Wasp* prior to Operation Calendar. J.G. Mejor in the front row, far right, and CO David Douglas Hamilton, front row, middle. (J.G. Mejor)

Spitfire taking off from USS *Wasp*, Operation Calendar, April 1942 (US National Archive)

the morning visit by the *Luftwaffe*. He was concerned that after over 3 hours in a cramped cockpit, stiff and with sore backsides, they might need to fight their way in. Fortunately the Germans had gone home by the time they arrived and 603 Squadron landed safely at Takali.

Group Captain 'Woody' Woodhall recalled the day these reinforcements arrived:

> However, the great day arrived [20 April] when our new Spitfires were expected. Naturally we had every available Hurricane and Spitfire ready to cover their landing. This they did so effectively that none of the new aircraft were lost from enemy action when within range of our fighter cover. Each flight was briefed to call me on a certain wireless channel when within range and I then detailed them to land at an appropriate aerodrome. We split these Spitfires between Luqa and Takali in order to facilitate their refuelling and rearming. An experienced pilot would be waiting to take over each Spitfire because the pilots who had flown them in would be tired and would not know the form.

Ray Hesselyn and Paul Brennan were watching the new arrivals from the bastions at Mdina. The latter remembered:

> Nobody could tell us when the new Spitfires were due but a whisper went round that the 20th was the day. By nine that morning Hess and I with a number of others had walked up to the bastions at Mdina and were eagerly looking westward. It was ten before we saw the new Spitfires sweep across Imtafa Hill and come into the circuit at Takali. As they passed above our heads someone shouted excitedly, 'Look, they have got four cannons'. Sure enough they had. They were a later Mark Vb Spitfire than those we had been used to. Squadron Leader Gracie who had gone to lead them in was in command of the new arrivals. Some of them clearly did

not know the form and had some difficulty in landing. There was a clear landing path but on either side there were bomb holes and some of the boys had difficulty in deciding exactly where to alight.

The pilots were taken to the officers' mess. On the way it became evident how much of a pounding Malta had experienced. There were parts of burnt-out aircraft everywhere: Spitfires, Hurricanes, Beaufighters, Marylands and a few German planes which had been shot down near the airfield. Everywhere there were bomb holes, craters, wreckage and battered buildings, some reduced to piles of rubble. The arrival of the Spitfires had not gone unnoticed by the Germans and it was not long before the first air-raid sirens were sounded. All of the airfields came under attack. Takali was hit first, then Luqa, Hal Far and Grand Harbour. The spectacle of witnessing such a staggering attack so shortly after arriving on the island was awesome. Many of the pilots had never heard the whistle of a bomb before and some had not seen enemy aircraft. The incredible spectacle was repeated later that afternoon and early evening. All hell broke loose and, in spite of strenuous efforts by the fighters and anti-aircraft guns, German Ju 87s and Ju 88s and escorting Me 109s managed to damage and destroy far too many of the newly arrived Spitfires on the ground. The blast pens were made of local stone or stacks of petrol tins filled with sand, and provided useful protection against cannon shells and blast from anything but a direct hit. They had no roof, however, and several aircraft received damage when rocks blown high into the air fell on them from above.

The Air Officer Commander, Air Marshal Sir Hugh Pugh Lloyd, went to the mess at Rabat with the Sector Commander, 'Woody' Woodhall, to welcome the new pilots and witnessed the raids. By the end of the day about 300 German and Italian bombers had been sent to Malta, mainly to destroy the newly arrived Spitfires. Many of the Spitfires were still being serviced before they could be flown again. Lloyd and Woodhall addressed the new pilots that evening, many of whom were speechless and had never seen anything like it. It had been a ferocious welcome to Malta. Woodhall recalled:

> That evening the AOC and I met the new arrivals and had a yarn with them in the mess at Rabat. It was just dark, I remember, and as he wound up by saying, 'You have come to a great little island and one of these days people will talk about Malta and you will be proud to say "I was there" when the Hun dropped a stick of bombs unpleasantly close'. We could hear the whistle of the bombs and then the explosions as each stick approached, until finally the last stick whistled over the roof and exploded at the bottom of the battlements. The AOC didn't bat an eyelid but I don't mind admitting that most of us, including the new pilots, wanted to get under something. I looked around at the startled and frightened faces and they were all looking at the AOC, who just repeated, 'I was there'. I think they realised what a man they had to lead them. After the AOC had left we all sat around on the balcony and I got to know them all, and I don't think I have ever been so bombarded with questions. I loved those evenings with the boys; no one who has not met them on their own ground, so to speak, can realise what a splendid mixture they are, of youth and commonsense, of naivety and guts, of humour and sadness and sentiment and thoughtfulness. In fact they are the cream of the earth.

The following morning the stark realisation of the ferocity of the attacks became apparent. Most of the Spitfires had been damaged and were unserviceable, some of the protective blast pens had collapsed under the weight of the bomb explosions and the planes had suffered shrapnel damage or been destroyed altogether. The bomb craters had been largely filled in overnight but they could only find six serviceable aircraft. Almost all of those flown in from the USS *Wasp* had been damaged or destroyed.

The following day, 22 April, Air Marshal Tedder sent a telegram to the Chief of Air Staff. It confirmed that after the arrival of the Spitfires from the USS *Wasp*, the *Luftwaffe* had attacked within 90 minutes and in three days had dropped over 500 tons of bombs on the airfields of Takali and Luqa. The German intention was to bring Malta to submission by air blockade, destroying the airfields, aircraft and equipment , along with the harbour facilities to prevent a convoy unloading. The defence of the island still only had six to eight Spitfires for each sortie, since nine had been destroyed on the ground and another twenty-nine rendered unserviceable by bomb damage in their blast pens. A further eight had been destroyed in combat, with most of the rest damaged in the aerial fighting. Further damage to the small number remaining was likely from taking off and landing among the bomb holes. The telegram ended by adding that it would not be possible to run a convoy to bring the vital supplies needed before the air situation was satisfactory, as it would be destroyed en route or in harbour. Malta needed 100 Spitfires a month. An abundance was necessary to hold the island, and after landing they must be put back in the air before the next raid arrived, or else face destruction on the ground.

Churchill again acted on the information and sent another message to Roosevelt:

> I am deeply anxious about Malta under the increasing bombardment of 450 first line German aircraft. If the island is to hold out until the June convoy, the earliest possible, it must have a continued flow of Spitfires. The last flying off from *Wasp* was the most successful although the enemy attacks broke up many after they had landed. We are using HMS *Eagle* to send in fifteen or so at a time. I shall be grateful if you will allow *Wasp* to do a second trip. Without this I fear Malta will be pounded to bits.

Roosevelt responded as Churchill had hoped on 25 April and confirmed that the *Wasp* could be made available for a second trip with Spitfires to Malta.

Churchill wrote to the Chief of the Air Staff the same day, 'Now that the President has agreed about *Wasp* let me know the programme for feeding Malta with Spitfires, week by week, during the next eight weeks'. On completion of the its first delivery of Spitfires, the USS *Wasp*, after a brief stop in Gibraltar, arrived back in the Clyde on 26 April. The code name given to the second attempt to deliver further Spitfires to Malta was Operation Bowery. It was clear that after the farce of the delivery of the first batch of planes, the reception arrangements for the second batch had to be improved. It was also evident that experienced pilots were required. This was not a criticism of Mejor necessarily, for he had been on operations with 132 Squadron at Peterhead, with over 50 hours on nearly thirty-five operations. It was more a criticism of some of the other pilots who did not have the same level of experience or were straight out of Operational Training Units, with no operational experience at all. Malta was no place for a beginner.

With the USS *Wasp* back on the Clyde, plans continued for Operation Bowery and the second delivery of Spitfires from her to Malta. Apart from the requirement for experienced pilots, plans were made to get experienced ground crews and spares through to the island by using the fast mine-layer HMS *Welshman*.

Since every single-engine fighter delivered to Malta for the previous twelve months had been flown in, there was no shortage of pilots, experienced or otherwise, for the few Spitfires available for operations at any time. As a result Mejor did not make his first operational flight from the island until 8 May, some eighteen days after his arrival, in the build-up to the second relief operation from the USS *Wasp*. By then he had been posted from 603 Squadron to 126 Squadron, originally under the command of Squadron Leader 'Jumbo' Gracie.

Gracie had returned to England to argue the case for more Spitfires to be flown to Malta and had led the new Spitfires from the USS *Wasp*. He had been replaced as 126 Squadron leader in late April by Flight Lieutenant A.R.H. 'Killer' Barton. 'Killer' was shot down five times and ended up destroying as many German planes as had knocked him down. Also with 126 Squadron were Flight Lieutenant Tim Johnston – known as Johnnie – Pilot Officer D.W. 'Mac' McLeod, Pilot Officer J.E. 'Jimmy' Peck, Pilot Officer Mike Graves, Pilot Officer B.H.E. 'Bis' Bisley, Pilot Officer 'Bill' Bailey, Flight Sergeant Eric 'Junior' Crist – or Chrissy – the Canadian, and Flight Sergeant 'Slim' Yarra, an Aussie.

One of Barton's first actions as squadron leader was to form an all-American 'B' Flight within the squadron led by Flight Lieutenant Jimmy Peck. He was joined by Jimmy's close friend, 'Mac' McLeod, and Pilot Officers Down, Reade Tilley and Booth. 'Killer' was known to favour the Americans as pilots and it helped with camaraderie that they were part of the same flight within the same squadron. Peck, who went on to win the DFC, and McLeod were the first Americans to shoot down an Me 109 over Malta: each had been successful on the same day, 24 March. A quiet, unassuming little fellow, Peck was in direct contrast to McLeod physically and lacked McLeod's wit, but they both formed an alliance with Johnnie Mejor, as did Reade Tilley when he joined. Tilley was not only a skilful and courageous pilot, but perhaps also the most striking-looking of all of them; he was tall, well built and invariably smart. Other American Eagle pilots such as McHan and Almos were posted into the flight from other squadrons and gave a good account of themselves.

Meanwhile preparations in Malta for the arrival of further Spitfires continued after the debacle following the first batch's landing. Every effort would be made to fly off the Spitfires earlier in the day, preferably before midday, so that they could be could be flown and landed on Malta before dark, reducing the risk of running into unseen bomb craters and holes in the gloom on arrival. Secondly, and almost too obviously, but still of the utmost importance, the Spitfires had to be serviceable in every respect before they were flown off the aircraft carrier and be ready to go into action immediately after landing on Malta, once they had been re-fuelled. Some of the Spitfires that had arrived on 20 April had apparently been in such a poor state of repair, that even though personnel worked on them through the night, they remained unserviceable the following morning. Guns were dirty and had not been synchronised – most of them had not been fired since they had been installed in the planes – and the radios often did not work. With aircraft in such short supply, and against such overwhelming odds, it was ridiculous that newly arrived Spitfires were kept on the ground for two or three days while they were being made serviceable.

The organisation on landing was also capable of improvement on that following the arrival of the first batch. Provided they arrived serviceable and in daylight, it was considered possible that the Spitfires could be put back into the air within 10 minutes of landing. To achieve this, five men were to be placed in each aircraft pen with an experienced pilot. He would be used to the fighting conditions over Malta, would have to be ready to jump into the cockpit when the Spitfire had been quickly serviced and turned around and then stay there in readiness for take-off. It was also the pilot's job to make sure each member of his team knew what he had to do to ensure this quick turn-around. The petrol was to be kept in 5-gallon tanks or tins protected by sandbags outside each aircraft pen because there were insufficient petrol bowsers. Each aircraft pen therefore contained all the necessary equipment and personnel to re-arm, re-fuel and service each aircraft. The long distance tanks, if they had been retained, would have to be removed. It would be equally essential to ensure a minimum delay between the landing of the Spitfire and its arrival at its allotted aircraft pen, where the experienced Malta-based pilot would take over. Each aircraft would be allocated a number on landing that corresponded to an aircraft pen. The aerodrome control officer would shout the number and a member of the ground crew would jump on the wing and direct the pilot to the appropriate aircraft pen. For it all to work, however, practice was needed, right down to the last detail. Nothing would be left to chance.

## 8 MAY 1942

On Malta, preparations for the second batch of Spitfires – which was expected the following day – continued, with all the pilots of the Malta-based squadrons in readiness at dawn to practise for the arrival of the reinforcements. Every pilot was allocated a pen and stayed there until lunch. It was a very busy day and a full dress rehearsal for the arrival of the reinforcement Spitfires the following day. Every detail of the plan and organisation was tested thoroughly. The Army was there in full force, with crater fillers, stretcher bearers, dispatch riders and Bren gun carriers that would haul any damaged aircraft out of the way.

Just after lunch the Ju 87s and Ju 88s came over, bombs screaming down, some chained together, and the whole place shook with the crash of explosions and continual bark of anti-aircraft fire in return. 'Woody' Woodhall, the Sector Commander, had sent all planes into the air. It was a hell of a fight. The Italians were bombing at the same time as the Germans, but it was their escort that Johnnie Mejor got caught up with. There were dogfights all around Takali, with Spitfires chasing Me 109s up into the sun while other Me 109s jumped them from other directions in a real free-for-all. Despite being outnumbered four or five to one, only one of the Hurricanes coming in to land was hit; the pilot crash-landed but was unhurt:

Log Book: Spitfire Vb – Interception Plot 50+ Island defence – ⌘
Me 109 destroyed. Yellow nose. Got burst at his No 2. Was jumped
at 17,000 feet by four Me 109s. Had no ammunition and was
forced to do dummy attacks.

That evening 'Killer' Barton gave the squadron a briefing:

Fellows, this is it. One half of the aircraft will land at Takali and
one half at Luqa. As you all know there are many pens built. Each
one of these pens will house an aircraft. At each pen there will be
a number of men, of whom one will be an experienced Malta
pilot. The minute the aircraft touches down he will be flagged
immediately into a pen in the dispersal area. Ground crew will
instantly tear off the long-range petrol tanks, another crewman
will begin pouring petrol from already handy five-gallon tins. Each
squadron will have a definite purpose. Our purpose will be to intercept enemy fighters. The positions of the other squadrons will be
varied. We will then attempt the diversion of the bombers from the
targets. The other aircraft on the island will be used in defending
you and the other squadrons in their efforts. In other words, the
success of the entire operation depends on you becoming immediately airborne. With units co-operating as usual and with good
luck, gentlemen, we can turn the tide of this, our little war. The
minute that our radar picks up a bomber strength building up
over Sicily, every aircraft will become airborne. Immediately upon
arrival at your pen, you will get the pilot out of the aircraft who
flew it in, put him to work in some handy way, get yourself into the
aircraft, strapped in and ready for instant take-off. When your flare
is given from the dispersal hut, each section will give it the gun and
take off. When your flare is given you will have a clear field. If you
should only have half a tank of petrol, take off anyway.

# 9 MAY 1942

At dawn the next morning, Squadron Leader 'Jumbo' Gracie again addressed all the pilots. He stood on the roof of a utility truck with the pilots, ground crew and soldiers lined up on the aerodrome in front of him. He spoke in the same strain as Barton had done the evening before and wished everyone good luck. Experienced pilots from Malta had been sent back to Gibraltar to meet up with the fleet and guide the new batch of Spitfires into Malta. Squadron Leader Stan Grant from 249 Squadron would lead the first batch of sixteen. They were to fly along the north coast of Algeria and Tunisia as far as Cap Bon, then head southeast to skirt around the enemy-held island of Pantelleria in the Sicilian channel before heading for Malta.

Oddly enough, the normal early morning routine of a raid by Ju 88s did not materialise; neither did marauding Me 109s. But by 10 a.m. the new boys started to arrive, coming in over Imtarfa Hill just as the first Me 109s also arrived. The Spitfires arrived in batches of twelve. All were down in half an hour. Me 109s shot up Hal Far and Luqa and managed to get a couple of the new boys who had not seen them. Sixty-odd Spitfires arrived, which was a colossal effort by everyone. A few Spitfires were ready again in 4 minutes, and the worst in 7 minutes. At just after 11 a.m. there was another alert and they all thought that this was it – the Germans were bound to know the time of the arrival of the Spitfires from their radar location and Kesselring was sure to try and catch them on the ground, just as he had done with the first batch before they could be re-fuelled and re-armed. There was to be no repeat this time though; the Spitfires were ready to fight.

Johnnie Mejor sat in the cockpit of the newly arrived Spitfire. He had shoved the new pilot officer bringing the plane to Malta into cover from the bullets and followed orders. One by one the reinforcement had made their landings, with much less opposition than had been expected. Mejor was ready. His plane had been re-fuelled. Any minute now the German bombers would arrive, any second the take-off flare would be seen. But he waited and waited, getting hotter and hotter in the sun. There was no raid, no bombers and the sky was empty. Suddenly, the all-clear siren was sounded. 'Surely not? It can't be,' he thought. Where were the German bombers?

Then they came. There was a far longer time interval between the arrival of the Spitfires and the attack when it came. The AA bursts pointed out around forty German fighters at 12,000ft and two red lights were fired from the wagon to signal the squadron to scramble. As he switched on, Mejor's airmen leapt to the starter trolley before his engine coughed twice and burst into life. Mejor did his cockpit checks again, lifted his thumb to the airmen and he was racing away in a dust cloud. One by one the Spitfires lifted from the ground and started to climb. A formation of twelve Ju 88s seemed to come out of a hole in the clear blue sky at around 17,000ft, dropping down in stages of 2,000 or 3,000ft at a time. Behind them and much higher were five Italian CANTs in perfect formation, and behind them in turn – and again higher – was their escort of forty to fifty fighters. They were such overwhelming odds:

Log Book: Spitfire Vc – Interception. Got behind five Cants. Could not see to fire. Good rear gunners, they bloody well hit me!

Another raid came in around 4.40 p.m. when there were signs of a further large formation of bombers assembling over Sicily. They bombed Takali, which made it necessary to switch the aircraft based there to Hal Far and Luqa. Two soldiers were killed in the bombing and one Spitfire was lost in the air with another two damaged, against enemy losses of four destroyed (including three of the Cants), nine probable kills and seven aircraft damaged. A dusk attack seemed inevitable but did not come, which to some was something of an anti-climax. That night, with only light raids, an exhausted Mejor was able to sleep for the first time in around 48 hours.

## 10 MAY 1942

Early in the morning of 10 May HMS *Welshman*, a fast minelayer, was due to make an unescorted run from Gibraltar into Malta. Its cargo included quantities of anti-aircraft ammunition, smoke canisters, aircraft engines, powdered milk, canned meat and dehydrated foods, together with 100 RAF technicians to help service the batch of Spitfires on the island. This day was seen as just as important as the day before when the new Spitfires had arrived.

Mejor was in readiness at 5 a.m. All his fellow pilots and airmen were still shattered from the day before. After a quick wash, with no shave and only cold water to wake himself up, he followed his CO downstairs by candlelight as the electric had failed again. Onto the bus, with no windows, the cold air woke him up further on a journey made more interesting by the large number of delayed action bombs dropped overnight by raiders. It was still dark and they could not see the bombs, but a crowd of bomb disposal boys were doing their best to remove them. Occasionally one would go off with a terrific roar and they had numerous shocks; as the morning wore on they got so used to the explosions they took little notice.

The day broke fine and clear, and began with an alert around 5.40 a.m. with forty-five fighters, although they were not scrambled to meet them as they stayed well away from the island. HMS *Welshman* arrived on time just after 6 a.m. and attacks on the valiant ship were expected and regarded as certain. Once again, though, Kesselring was not running to form and kept the bombers away. There was a further alert at 8.20 a.m. when thirty-two fighters came over but again the defenders refused to be drawn.

But at 10 a.m. there were signs of the bombers over Sicily and soon the Ju 88s and Ju 87s arrived and dived down on HMS *Welshman*. A grey-green smokescreen spread wide over Grand Harbour as they attempted to cover the target area and shield the ship. The AA barrage put up was tremendous, spattering the blue sky with shell bursts, and into this inferno dived the German bombers, with Spitfires behind them. It seemed incredible, with Spitfires everywhere chasing bombers, with the constant risk of collision due to the number of aircraft. A Ju 87 was hit, dropped like a stone, then another and another; sometimes two or three at a time. More Spitfires dived into the fray, searching, plunging, wheeling and screaming. Then a Spitfire was hit, split in two, broken by a bursting shell, but a parachute emerged and opened in the maelstrom, floating gently downwards.

From the ground, thousands of civilians could see the spectacular air battle developing over Grand Harbour and they cheered each time a German was hit. The spectacle was also witnessed by the ground crews at the airfields, who threw their tools, hats, rifles and anything else they could lay their hands on into the air when they saw any German in flames or crash.

The CO, Squadron Leader Barton, led a flight of five Spitfires to attack the bombers. Flight Sergeant Schade claimed one Ju 88 destroyed after it burst into flames, Pilot Officer J. Bailey claimed a further Ju 87 and Pilot Officer Mike Graves a Ju 88 shot down and a Ju 87 probably hit. Barton also claimed an escorting Me 109 shot down. Flight Lieutenant Jimmy Peck led his 'American' flight with Mejor off the Sicilian coast to meet returning stragglers and achieved further success – Sergeant A. Goldsmith claimed an Me 109 destroyed (seen diving away in flames), Wally Milner also had a probable kill and Jimmy Peck and Reade Tilley both claimed damaged Me 109s. As his section returned to Malta, more bombers were sighted and Peck shot down a further Ju 87 while Mejor claimed a Ju 88 as a probable:

Log Book: Spitfire Vc – Island Defence. ⚡ Ju 88 probable. Killed
gunner. Range about 50 yards. Large pieces came away. Many
strikes. Port engine was on fire and heavy smoke. Went down
steeply towards sea. Burst at Ju 87 and Me 109. No results.

After a minor alert at midday, the *Luftwaffe* returned at 2 p.m.
with seven Ju 88s escorted by about thirty Me 109s, again concentrating on Grand Harbour and the *Welshman*. The squadron had
just got down and Mejor was in a queue of airmen waiting for a
plate of food and a mug of tea when the scramble came again.
Two more red flares and he was away, but he was the only one to
get back up and had a narrow escape flying his second sortie of
the day:

Log Book: Spitfire Vc – Island defence. Ran into squadron of
Me 109s when alone and got badly shot up. Short bursts of 2 seconds at two Me109s. Forced to break each time Me 109s on my
tail. Twenty-eight holes in my aircraft!

As evening approached another raid began to build up on the radar
screens. Again, 126 Squadron was scrambled to meet the incoming raid – this time seven aircraft including Mejor were up along
with ten Spitfires from 601 Squadron, seven from 185 Squadron,
eight from 249 Squadron and ten from 603 Squadron. The
Spitfires scrambled as the raid approached and all intercepted
the German aircraft in the second wave. Flight Sergeant Milner
and Pilot Officer Tilley each claimed an Me 109 destroyed and
Mejor was attacking another Ju 87 which he claimed as destroyed
when he too was shot down:

Log Book: Spitfire Vb – Island defence. ⚡ Ju 87 probable – strikes
on rear gunner and seen along port wing and fuselage. Range
50 yards. Me 109 hit me from behind and below. Engine caught

fire and controls jammed. Kite turned upside down. Bailed out at 2,000ft and 4–6 miles off the coast. I had no time to send a mayday call and bailed out into the sea. I saw two plane crashes close together which I think were my Spitfire and the Ju 87 I shot down, but I was only credited with a third of a kill because I couldn't be sure that my target was the one that hit the water. I was lucky to be picked up by HSL107 who were looking for another pilot who had sent a mayday. They didn't find him but found me instead.

Mejor had been done by the sucker punch; concentrating on getting the Ju 87, he had lost concentration and taken his eye off his mirror and the rear when he was hit by one of the Me 109 escort. The next instant, without warning, he could hear and feel cannon shells exploding in the rear of the Spitfire. He instinctively kicked the rudder as the first cannon shell exploded but the Spitfire did not respond. A sensation of insignificance, resignation and sheer bloody mindedness was then overtaken by fear and fate. He needed to get out. He felt trapped in the blazing Spitfire. He thought to himself, 'What's the routine? Remember, for Christ sake, remember the drill.' Disorientated and upside down, he struggled to get free, still stuck in his seat, squirming against the straps to get out. Then he remembered to press the harness release and shove the canopy back. There was a sudden blast of cool rushing air, then he was out and down, down and away from the burning plane. He pulled the rip cord of the parachute. All was quiet and peaceful as he drifted down to the sea about 5 miles off the coast. What next?

## 'I WISH I HAD YOUR WINGS'

Luckily, although Mejor had not had a chance to send a mayday, he had been spotted coming down. HSL 107, an Air Sea Rescue launch based at Kalafrana, was sent out to rescue another pilot, but found him instead. They soon found a patch of oil and wreckage that marked where his Spitfire and the Ju 87 had entered the water, but there was no sign of a spreading patch of the pea-green fluorescent dye carried by the pilots as markers. This in itself was a good sign as it meant that he had not gone down with the Spitfire, and anyway he had been seen to bail out. The probability was that he had drifted in the wind on his way down.

As he had hit the sea, Mejor had attempted to inflate his dinghy before releasing his parachute, which soon began to sink. He let go of the dinghy to release the parachute but was not quick enough to grab the dinghy before that too sank, so all he had for buoyancy was his Mae West life jacket. Alone and cold, and getting colder, in the sea off Malta was not his idea of fun. He was soon joined by a flock of sea gulls and recalled years later that he struck up a conversation with one in particular, 'Oh how I wish I had your wings', and thought how he could have done with them at that very moment! After what seemed like several hours, but what was actually no more than an hour, HSL 107 found Mejor. The gulls and his Mae West had given away his position, but even after only an hour in the water he was exhausted and suffering from cramp. He was unable to help himself so the crew got him aboard with some difficulty, stripped off his Mae West and jacket and carried him below. After a few minutes' massage and a welcome brandy, some sort of circulation returned. He was sick from the combination of seawater and brandy, but was alive – very lucky to be alive. He was taken back to Malta in the comparative warmth of the launch's cabin and by evening he was returned to the squadron.

That night, Rome Radio tried to claim that forty-seven Spitfires had been destroyed and a strong force had been attacked in Grand Harbour. In fact only three Spitfires had been lost, two of the pilots – including Mejor – were safe, and the strong force in the harbour was just HMS *Welshman* which had left under cover of darkness. The RAF, with the reinforcements flown in from the USS *Wasp*, had regained air superiority and 10 May could justifiably be claimed as a major turning point in the air battle for Malta.

Thousands of Maltese had witnessed the air battles. When evening came, the Maltese knew the British had won a great victory and the gloom and depression which had hung over the island for so long had been lifted.

# 4

# Malta, May to August 1942: the 'Dog' and Sheer Bloody Exhaustion

'Malta Dog' was a debilitating condition that threatened to undermine the effectiveness of the island's fighting forces. The unpleasant form of dysentery attacked suddenly and weakened the constitution of anyone already significantly underweight due to reduced rations. Sufferers could be confined to bed for several days, unable to return to duties until their condition stabilised.

For about a fortnight Mejor had been feeling low with the symptoms of the 'Dog' – all food tasted like fat and was difficult to swallow, giving him severe stomach cramps. In addition, any prolonged attack of the 'Dog' was both painful and exhausting, and the fact it that seemed to be always with him meant that with him bailing out and needing recuperation, he was stood down for a week and did not fly again until th 17 May.

Days off were priceless but Mejor's were a necessity. It was nigh on impossible for him to relax due to the constant air attacks and warnings. Late one afternoon he was still dressed in his pyjamas, lying on a sofa in the bar with a greatcoat around him. He was shivering and then sweating again, sunbathing on the flat roof outside to get rid of the dreadful fits of icy fever. There was no relief from the pains in his stomach which clenched his intestines, or the splitting headaches. He was clearly unfit to fly, and he was not the only one. The CO, Barton, was also laid low, as was Mike Graves. Barton was a sight to behold, shuffling around the dusty floor in his flying boots and old silk dressing gown. Graves had also succumbed to the 'Dog' but had been on duty the day before, shooting down a Ju 88, but his Spitfire flew through the disintegrating wreckage and blew up. Graves had managed to bail out but was a little shaken up, to say the least.

With no respite, constant air attacks, a persistent pain in his head and constant cramps in his stomach, Mejor was sent to the St Paul's Bay rest camp and decided to starve himself for four days to try and rid himself of the dreaded 'Dog'. He tried to forget the war.

The rest camp was a haven, close to the water, with a swimming platform and silver shimmering water – inviting and relaxing. Boats rocked gently, water smacking against their sides, and the sun kept him warm and relaxed. He slept a lot, and did not eat:

**17 May 1942**
Log Book – Spitfire Interception Fighter Sweep – Me109s came in at 23,000ft. Went out immediately.

If it had not been for the three replacement pilots transferred from 603 Squadron to cover those suffering still from the 'Dog', the squadron would have been understrength.

It was clear, however, that Mejor was still not right, even after his break and recuperation. Despite declaring himself fit to fly, on landing he was again doubled up in agony with stomach cramps. He continued to try and fly. There was no choice as some of the new boys did not have enough experience and there was no such thing as training flights to get them used to operations.

On 19 May more Spitfires arrived under Operation LB – seventeen. They were flown in from HMS *Eagle*, the backlog of Spitfires left behind in Gibraltar for various reasons after the recent ferry operations. Squadron Leader 'Laddie' Lucas had been flown back to Gibraltar with a couple of experienced flight commanders, Buck McNair and Raoul 'Daddo' Langlois, who led them into Malta.

The arrival of this latest Spitfire reinforcement coincided with a major withdrawal of *Luftwaffe* forces from Sicily for service on the Russian Front, which caused a sudden and most noticeable falling away in air activity over Malta. One Me 109 Group and two Ju 88 Groups had been transferred to Russia, leaving only the Me 109s of 11 Jagdgeschwader (JG) 53 and the Ju 88s of Kampfgruppen (KGr) 606 and KGr 806, plus the Italian *Regia Aeronautica* units reinforced from the Italian mainland, but this did

not mean that the island was out of the woods. It was still peril-
ously short of supplies.

## 23 MAY 1942

Sent up to intercept five Cant Z1007s escorted by sixteen Reggiane
Re 2001s and four Me 109s from JG 53 that were bombing Takali,
Paddy Schade was also back in the air after recovering from his
arm wound. He tangled with the Me 109s, 'Jumped 4 Me 109s
about ten miles north of Grand Harbour, one destroyed and one
probable'. Mejor also flew but was unable to make a claim:

> Log Book – Spitfire Scramble – Attacked five Cants. My No's 2, 3
> and 4 had lost me. Return fire from gunners. Three second burst
> 200 yards dead astern on port one. Three Reggianes attacked from
> port bow above. Turned in head-on firing at leader of formation.
> Saw no results.

Around this time Group Captain 'Woody' Woodhall, the senior
controller, did the rounds of all the airfields with some long-awaited
good news. A small, wiry middle-aged man who wore shorts much
too big for him, his khaki shirt bore an impressive array of ranks,
while below his Wings were two full rows of medals that testified to
his huge experience. Gathering around as requested, Mejor wondered what on earth could be the news. 'Well we've made a decision
about you fellows,' Woodhall started mischievously:

> You all know that the normal overseas tour of duty is two to three
> years and that's what you expected when you all arrived here. The
> intensity of the fighting in Malta is now officially recognised and
> it has been decided to give you a rest in three months' time. You
> are not going to be sent to the Middle East, you will be sent back

to England. You have all done a fine job and we would love to give you a rest right now if we could, but of course, you realise that since we are besieged here, the manner of your replacements will depend on seats available in transit planes. We are however going to start sending pilots home straight away. Pilots who have been here 6 months already will be leaving tonight or as soon as we can arrange seats. After that 3 months will be considered a full Malta tour for fighter pilots.

Most of them were astonished by this news, an absolute bolt from the blue. Three months, 'Woody' had said. Mejor immediately started to work out how long he had been there – five weeks, that was all. Only five weeks. It seemed impossible, yet seemed almost a lifetime. He had only done a third of his duty period and still had two months more. What chance was there of staying alive? Little or none, he thought, he would never be able to do it. Self-doubt began to creep in. He was tired, now; more than tired, absolutely shattered, and wrecked by the 'Dog'.

## 31 MAY 1942

Log Book – Spitfire Scramble. Wizard scrap. Had fight with four Eyeties 20 miles off Sicily.

The last few days of May were so quiet that they could afford to send off sections on practice flying and many of the new arrivals went up with the old hands. For those who had been on Malta from the time the first Spitfires arrived, it presented a striking con-trast to the conditions which had existed beforehand. Indeed, had anybody told them a few weeks earlier that they would be practice flying by the end of May, they would have been told where to go. But it had happened and that was all the more remarkable.

The CO, 'Sailor' Barton, was sent back to Gibraltar by 'Woody' Woodhall, along with Jimmy Peck and Johnnie Plagis, as experienced flight leaders to bring the next batch of Spitfires in as part of Operation Style. A further thirty-two Spitfires would be dispatched from HMS *Eagle*. 'Sailor', or 'Admiral' as he had become known, was a great character and a magnificent leader, albeit unorthodox. Mejor and he got on. He was also a good friend of Woodhall, who had sent him back to Gibraltar to lead these Spitfires into Malta. They had to wait a few days and stayed in the Rock Hotel on Gibraltar. They naturally and excusably arrived in a rather untidy and shabby condition, as they had only been allowed to bring 45lb of kit from England in the first place. Thanks to losses from bombing and pilfering, the pilots rarely had one decent uniform between them and as it was impossible to replace on Malta, they would have to replace them if they got a chance on Gibraltar. Until they could, their dress was fancy to say the least.

During their first dinner (their first decent meal for weeks), an officious wing commander who had been living in ease and comfort in Gibraltar under almost peacetime conditions, sent a waiter to ask 'Admiral' to report to him at his table, whereupon, in public, he ran him down for being improperly dressed. The CO took it, but humorously told Woody about the incident on his return to Malta, 'I was only wearing one khaki sock, one blue one, khaki slacks, a blue tunic and scarf. It was all I had to wear and the blighter didn't even have Wings on his chest. It makes you think, doesn't it?'. 'Woody' was furious when he found out about the public admonishment and tried to locate the said wing commander when he went back through Gibraltar in July. It is perhaps as well that he did not find him!

## JUNE 1942

The lull in enemy air activity continued, but the supply situation was becoming critical as there had been no convoy to Malta since March, before 603 or 126 Squadron had arrived on Malta. Fuel and ammunition for the aircraft was being brought in by submarines but a substantial convoy was required if the island was to survive. While the general situation in the air had eased, Me 109s still swept in to draw up the Spitfires. The squadrons were, in general, well equipped and organised, with a surplus of pilots, which meant that the duty rota allowed periods of rest every few days.

Mejor was still wrecked by the 'Dog', absolutely exhausted and was confined to hospital at Imtarfa to try and recover.

His daughter recalled to me:

My father was grounded and sent into hospital because he had red spots floating over his pupils. He was exhausted, but would never have said a word. He was furious to be sent off to hospital, basically for a rest. Whilst in there they admitted a Ju 88 pilot. My father's German was fluent and they struck up conversation.

The hospital authorities didn't worry about the German prisoners escaping; they were afraid of the Maltese, who would have been very happy to get hold of them.

They had all been living and fighting under a huge strain. The poor quality of the food had been noticed at first but was now beginning to take effect. Everyone was showing and feeling the pinch. Nothing was obtainable except the basic rations. Even the black market 'titbits' disappeared, down to the local oranges which were normally so juicy but were in short supply. There had been the occasional supply of figs, plums and other fruit and some eggs, but all these had long gone. Their daily diet was a slice and a half of very poor bread with jam for breakfast, bully beef for lunch with one slice of bread and the same fare for dinner. And that was assuming your stomach could take it and you didn't have the 'Dog'. There was sugar for every meal but margarine only every two or three days. Even the drinking water, lighting and heating were rationed. In fact everything was rationed. The supply of coke, coal and paraffin would last for a few more weeks but then they would have to salvage it from the ships sunk in Grand Harbour and also use salvaged wood for firewood. All the things taken for granted began to close down; the making of beer required coal, so none had been made for months. Even the water depended on coal and, as there was no electricity or gas, food had to be heated with wood salvaged from bombed out houses. The RAF messes had burnt used aeroplane oil for months and they had got used to the strong sooty, oily flavour of food and tea. A crashed aeroplane was a windfall as the oil would provide an extra hot drink for a day or so. Everyone was living on the subsistence level and only a convoy could remedy the situation.

They joked about the siege in a blatant manner. Their plight was distressing but everyone accepted it with philosophical fortitude. Rats were for sale at one shilling each, sparrows five shillings a pair, and mice were ninepence. To joke about it was the only thing to do. The cheerfulness of the Maltese and the garrison was remarkable. Thus Malta was faced with the prospect of starvation and from a lack of equipment could be forced to surrender. The middle of August was set as starvation date unless a convoy could get through.

After nearly three weeks in Imtarfa, Mejor was discharged and was back with 126 Squadron. He had missed a double attempt to get merchant ships into Malta but his CO had been heavily involved. 'Sailor' Barton recalled the events of 15 June:

One convoy left Alexandria codenamed 'Alex' and one left Gibraltar codenamed 'UK', once and for all to re-supply the island. However, although the Italian fleet had returned to base after a severe pummelling from our bombers, 'Alex', after heavy losses and out of ammunition, turned back for Egypt although it had just become within range of the Malta fighters. 'UK' continued to Malta. No. 126 and 601 Squadron Spitfires were fitted with Hurricane long-range tanks under the belly so that they could protect 'UK' once their protective umbrella of ships had to return to Gibraltar and before the Takali and Hal Far boys could protect them at about 70 miles out. These tanks effectively doubled the range to 140 miles. Only two supply ships got through, although there was no shipping loss once the Spitfires from Malta were able to give cover. Orders were: four Spitfires over the convoy, four Spitfires on route and four Spitfires returning – a continuous rotation. Four Spitfires against about 500! Orders also said: The four Spitfires over the convoy must not leave until relieved. If you ran out of fuel you had to ditch – effectively a death sentence!

From the moment Spitfires were able to provide cover over what remained of Convoy 'UK' there were no further losses, but one of the merchant ships had to be sunk by our own. There was talk of them swimming out and helping push her in, but this was quickly dismissed. After such heroic efforts and so close to Malta, it seemed tragic to see her put under the water so close to her objective. Thousands watched the two surviving merchantmen enter Grand Harbour late in the afternoon on the 15th, both ships battered and severely damaged. There was scarcely a cheer; it was victory to get the two through of sorts but it was more an occasion for deep reverence than one of joy. All of the effort in likewise getting Convoy 'Alex' close to Malta and also within striking distance proved to be in vain. It had used up so much of its anti-aircraft ammunition that it was ordered back to Alexandria. Of a total of 17 merchant ships that had tried to get to Malta, only two succeeded and their cargo could only provide a temporary respite

**20 June 1942**
Log Book – Spitfire Air test – fired at two Me 109s saw no results

**20 June 1942**
Log Book – Spitfire Escort for Baltimores and Beauforts

**20 June 1942**
Log Book – Spitfire Scramble – saw nothing

Towards the end of June, an event was aimed at marking with a simple ceremony the apparent victory over the German and Italian forces in Sicily and the successful arrival of the two ships in the latest convoy. It seemed that these events warranted a display, with Lord Gort holding an Investiture and decorating some of the pilots who had fought so valiantly. It also meant that the garrison and Maltese people could see and acclaim their heroes, with many airmen being awarded medals. There was some concern over the safety of any crowd from bombing attacks because they would need to assemble in front of the Castille facing the Square in Valletta to witness the ceremony, but it went ahead nevertheless. Facing Lord Gort were ranks of pilots, soldiers and sailors, with thousands of Maltese and the garrison there to witness the event and hail their heroes. It was left to Sir Hugh Pugh Lloyd to read the citations for each award for the airmen. 'Four enemy aircraft destroyed for one, eight for another, rescuing a crew from a burning plane, re-fuelling aircraft under fire, sinking two merchant ships' and so on. Each pilot, soldier and sailor was acclaimed, applauded and cheered as they climbed the steps to collect their awards.

It was also significant that pilots from every corner of the Commonwealth and Empire, and the USA, featured in the ceremony. Names such as James, Legge and Buchanan had come from Rhodesia; Middlemiss, Verrol, Jones, Williams, Buerling, Linton and MacNair from Canada; Yarra, Brennan, Copp, Mayall and Tweedale from Australia; Rae, Dickson and Hesselyn from New Zealand; and Peck, Tilly, Coffin, Junior, and MacLeod from the USA.

There were others. MacQueen, McNamara and Allardyce, who had been lost in the fighting. Bisdee and Delara, who had been pulled from the sea. Turner, Tayleur, Lee, Sluggett, Smith Barclay-Hill and the Squadron CO, David Douglas-Hamilton, Gilbert, Shaw, Barnham, Ferraby, Allen, Hurst, Lloyd, Graves, West, Lucas, Goldsmith, Andrews, Lawrence, Stenberg and Reid. Watts, Johnson, Grant, Cormack and 'Timber' Woods. Barnfather, Daddo-Langlois 'Daddy Longlegs', Holdsworth, Slade and Heppel – who had been shot down coming into land and whose parachute had only just deployed before he hit the ground – and lastly, Reid, Mejor, Mitchell, Hutchison, Noble and Hetherington.

With so many names and so many awards it was both a poignant and moving ceremony, notable also for those no longer there or still fighting, protecting the island from further attacks.

July marked an increase in air attacks once more and a new offensive from the Germans and Italians. To give the reader an idea of the increased air attacks and intensity, I have listed Mejor's log book entries for July below and left them mainly without narrative. To me, they speak for themselves.

## JULY 1942

### 3 July 1942

Log Book – Spitfire Scramble – Intercepted Me 109s South of Takali. We attacked from quarter astern but they dived away too fast for us. Three second burst at 300 yards no result.

### 3 July 1942

Log Book – Spitfire Scramble – three Cants and Squadron of Macchi 202s – My cannons jammed, so did Jimmy Peck's. Too bad. Had nice fight with the Macchi 202's dim wits.

### 3 July 1942

Log Book – Spitfire Scramble – 109s 30,000ft – we could not get up in time.

### 5th July 1942

Log Book – Spitfire Scramble – 109s came in 28,000ft and put their noses down across the island. We sighted one at 9 o'clock and turned into him but he pressed the tit. Told to pancake friendly aircraft.

### 5 July 1942

Log Book – Spitfire Scramble – Eyetie big and little jobs angels high. We got to 27,000ft but they turned back without making landfall.

### 5 July 1942

Log Book – Spitfire Scramble – ⚐ Me 109 yellow nose probable. We attacked from very close and saw strikes on cockpit. Piece dropped off starboard wing and he poured oil and smoke and went down on his back. His No. 2 attacked from line astern but we broke with lots of skid. He went nose down for home. We found Ken Evans scrapping with four Me 109s – they cleared off.

### 7 July 1942

Log Book – Spitfire Scramble – ⚐ Me 109 yellow nose destroyed and ⚐ Ju 88 damaged. Jimmy Peck attacked first but cannons would not work. Me 109 flying 1,000ft to port of three Ju 88s. I took Jimmy's place and fired from 100 yards. He poured black oil and smoke and spun down leaving a very long trail down. We peeled off and went into the Ju 88s from astern. I took port one and saw strikes on the side of the fuselage by wing roots. He turned away from formation. The rear gunners poured tracer at us and we were forced to break off.

**7 July 1942**
Log Book – Spitfire Scramble – detailed high cover for Me 109s – We sighted and attacked. I saw no results.

**9 July 1942**
Log Book – Spitfire Scramble – Got jumped by Me 109s. Section got split up. Got jumped again while alone at 28,000ft, saw them just in time.

**9 July 1942**
Log Book – Spitfire Air Sea Rescue search – Looking for P O Hicks with Reade Tilley. No sign of him. I found an abandoned dinghy. Hicky bought it.

**9 July 1942**
Log Book – Spitfire Scramble – ⊞ Ju 88 destroyed. Fired from beam passing quarter astern. It blew up and tail came off. Two burning chutes. Reade Tilley got first, I got second and F/Lt Rowe got third.

**11 July 1942**
Log Book – Spitfire Scramble – ⊞ Ju 88 destroyed shared with CO Squadron Leader Winfield. We attacked formation of Ju 88s and Me 109s. Heavy black oil and smoke from both engines. Confirmed by Y service as blood wagon. Looked for them.

**11 July 1942**
Log Book – Spitfire Scramble – got frost bite. Attacked formation of about 30–40 Ju 88s and Me 109s with S/Ldr Winfield. Gave

an 88 two bursts but had to break as 109s were playing behind us. We nearly bought it. Lost height. Ring twitch!

**13 July 1942**
Log Book – Spitfire Scramble – Attacked 88s but only had short burst as 109s on my tail. Had three short squirts at 109s during the fight but saw no result.

**13 July 1942**
Log Book – Spitfire Scramble – Few 88s bags of 109s and Macchis. Attacked 109s. Had super dogfight with two. Was separated from others and attacked two Me 109s about 10 miles N of Island. Very foxy blighters. Another Spit came to help and they beat it.

**15 July 1942**
Log Book – Spitfire Scramble – forced to land, big ends gone in engine.

Arriving in Gibraltar at the same time as Mejor was down with the 'Dog' again on Malta were the next batch of pilots to be flown into Malta from HMS *Eagle*. Among them was Sergeant Allan Scott. He and Mejor would become good friends on the island as they both joined 1435 Squadron. Scott takes up his recollection of his posting and flight to Malta:

As we disembarked from the *Empire Darwin*, Gibraltar was an amazing sight to new eyes. Its huge rock towered above us for the whole length of our walk from the docks to the block of rooms that was to be our accommodation until the next leg to Malta. All the pilots were housed here and each had his own room, a big improvement on the steel deck of the hold, but my first taste of luxury was in the form of a deep, deep bath. In Gibraltar our orders were to fly to Malta a contingent of 36 Spitfires off the carrier HMS *Eagle*.

They were given their orders and an information card, which advised:

Take-off as normal except (a) Throttle fully open; (b) Tail trim to central position; (c) Cold air; (d) See that knurled nut on throttle quadrant is firm. Formation: Join up as soon as possible in predetermined positions. WIDE FORMATION. Fly on overload tank until it runs dry then switch on main tanks and switch off overload tank. Note: Jettison overload tank if necessary if EMPTY. Gives extra 45 miles endurance. Maintain strict RT silence after leaving carrier. Only transmit in emergency. IFF on an ETA minus 30 minutes, approximately 90 miles from destination. Carrier call sign 'PYFFO'. If separated or lost: On last leg head north. Turn east on reaching land (Sicily) and follow coast to easternmost point, then set compass to 222 degrees (M) for destination. Don't Flap or Worry.

Scott recalled:

We were RAF pilots of course, not naval pilots, and had never taken off from a carrier. Positioned at the end of the deck with engines running and holding with brakes on, we kept our eyes fixed on the 'bats' (naval crewmen with batons). He would circle his 'bats' to indicate for us to open the throttle and would keep circling these 'bats' until he knew the revs were high enough to wave us away. When it was my turn I was convinced the nose of the Spitfire would hit the deck but blindly kept opening the throttle until he waved me forward, and I took the brakes off and started my run with throttle now fully open. Looking at the left white line under the cannon to keep me straight, I soon came up level and followed the centre line until at last and gratefully I was airborne and staggering over the bow. Once airborne, the flaps were lowered and the blocks fell away and with flaps raised again the Spitfire was clean and ready to fly.

Not all take-offs were successful. One pilot must have lost his nerve and failed to open the throttle for full power. He foundered and fell off the bow. Perhaps unnerved by seeing the Spitfire go over the edge, a second Spitfire got halfway down his run, closed the throttle and braked too hard and fast and, with hard right rudder applied, wrapped himself round a Bofors gun, much to the displeasure of the sailors manning it. They had to jump for their lives into the sea. The Spitfire was pushed overboard and the pilot, an Australian, was visibly upset and shaken, not by what had happened, but for the loss of the hoard of cigarettes he had stashed behind his seat!

Climbing away from the *Eagle* and now in some sort of formation, we set course for Malta. It was not all plain sailing, or should I say flying. About halfway and just to the right of our flight path was the island of Pantelleria, where there were German Me 109s based. We had enough fuel to fly to Malta and could not afford to get into a dogfight. It was a long anxious moment or two creeping past that island with all of us tense and sweating. We continued our flight and we made it, only to discover the island was in the middle of an air raid and that we were in a circuit to land, but with Me109s attacking the very airfield where we were supposed to land. Short of fuel, desperate to land and with an Me 109 on my tail, there was no time to put the undercarriage back up. I heaved the Spitfire into the tightest turn I have ever made in my life, the adrenalin gripping my body and helping me to evade his attack. He missed. I was able to out-turn him and shake him off. Only then could I attempt another landing. I managed it, aiming towards a pen, parked hurriedly, climbed out and dashed to the slit trench for safety. I was amazed to turn and see my Spitfire already being re-fuelled by a string of men, army, navy and air force, who were passing tins of petrol from hand to hand and then up to the 'Erk' who were straddling the fuselage as though riding on horseback. Desperate to get the Spitfire ready for the next scramble, he was pouring the petrol into a large funnel to fill the tank. I had landed at Takali – what a welcome to Malta!

Scott was posted to 603 Squadron but was only with them a few days before 603 was disbanded and 1435 Flight, later 1435 Squadron, formed, based at Luqa. He would spend his tour on Malta with 1435 Squadron.

## 1435 SQUADRON, JULY 1942

Their CO at the newly formed 1435 Squadron was Squadron Leader Tony Lovell, who had returned to Malta from his trip to Gibraltar. Among the other pilots posted to 1435 Squadron were Flight Lieutenants Halford and MacLeod, who would be the flight commanders, and experienced Malta pilots Johnnie Mejor, Flight Sergeant Vineyard and MacNamara from 185 Squadron, Pilot Officers Latimer and Baxter from 249 Squadron, Flight Sergeants Ron Stevenson and John Pinney and Sergeants Colin Wood, Wally Shepherd, Don Hubbard and Allan Scott.

The reinforcements meant some of the more exhausted pilots could be released back to the UK in line with the new 'three-month tour on Malta was enough for anyone' rule. Scotty and Mejor immediately formed a friendship. They looked after each other when they flew together and they got on well on the ground. It was a friendship that would last a lifetime. Perhaps it was Mejor's Scottish influence through his Scottish mother and Scott's own Scottish upbringing that enabled them to get on. 'Pugnacious and fiery character Johnnie was, always twirling his moustache, he was never prepared to take any rubbish from anyone, but always retained a wicked sense of humour even in those dark days in Malta,' Scott recalls.

Scott also remembers their CO, Tony Lovell:

He was very young, only 22 years old, but was already a Battle of Britain veteran having flown with 41 Squadron at Hornchurch, and knew the AOC Air Vice Marshal Park as a result. He was a slight, quiet man and deeply religious, he would say prayers every morning and could well have ended up as a Roman Catholic priest or in the Church for his faith and belief. At times he could be quite intense and a little highly strung, but he was good man and a good leader and already had the DFC.

**28 July 1942**
Log Book – Spitfire Scramble – Cruised about between Sicily and Malta at 28,000ft. CO and self were alone but neither saw anything.

**28 July 1942**
Log Book – Spitfire Scramble – CO and self only ones serviceable. Patrolled 'water babies'. Plot 30+ saw four Ju 88s going like hell. Four Me109s came towards us and we turned in but they turned back. Saw Ju 88 crash in the drink.

Mejor and Squadron Leader Lovell were ordered to patrol and orbit over minesweepers, hence the reference to 'water babies', and though they saw the bombers and escorting fighters, and chased and turned into them, they could not leave the minesweepers.

**28 July 1942**
Log Book – Spitfire Scramble – 卐 Ju 88 shared with CO W/Cdr Stainforth. 126 got the rest. All bombers shot down.

In the late afternoon, five Spitfires from 185 Squadron were ordered to patrol the north of the island and were joined just after 5 p.m. by sixteen more, eight from 1435 Squadron and eight from 126 Squadron. They intercepted three Ju 88s as they approached Hal Far. The first two were attacked by several pilots and went down quickly, one in flames and the other trailing white smoke which developed into a full fire before it hit the sea. The third was attacked by Pilot Officer Rod Smith from 126 Squadron and Mejor, Tony Lovell and Wing Commander Stainforth – who was CO of a Beaufighter night fighter unit and had borrowed a Spitfire to come along for the ride:

Intercepted three escorted Ju 88s heading west over Kalafrana Bay at the same height, we turned left into them and this time I was on the side furthest away and last into them. One of the Me 109 escort came right down among us blazing away but we ignored him. As was common, most of our pilots attacked the nearest 88, the one on the left-hand side of their formation, and a couple of them attacked the one in the centre. Both of them caught fire and went down in seconds. I flew across and opened fire on the far side, which no one else had attacked. The port engine of the 88 caught fire immediately and I carried my aim into the port wing root and then the fuselage and the starboard engine. The aircraft headed downwards and I kept firing for the full 12 seconds. Finally the engines came out, the wings fell off and all the burning pieces fell like a shower of golden rain. I was amazed to find later that three of the crew got out; they must have been quick off the mark, perhaps put on their toes by the other two Ju 88s going down seconds before.

**30 July 1942**
Log Book – Spitfire Scramble – Got jumped at 26,000ft by six Me 109s, had dogfight for about a minute and they left us. Woods bought it. 88s turned back without making landfall.

Just before 8 a.m., 1435 Squadron was scrambled to meet a reported fighter sweep of about twenty Me 109s and six Macchis. They were jumped by what they thought were ten Me 109s at 26,000ft around 10 miles north of Grand Harbour, but the attack included the Italian Macchis as it was the Italians who claimed two Spitfires shot down. Only one Spitfire actually fell; Sergeant Colin Wood, a New Zealander, was killed when his aircraft went into the sea off St Paul's Bay.

Four Spitfires from 126 Squadron were sent out to search for the missing pilot but nothing was sighted other than an oil patch when they were vectored north-east of St Paul's Bay.

Allan Scott also recalls the ferocity of one of the attacks, having just arrived on the island:

We were scrambled nearly every day to engage the bombers and escorting Me 109s as they approached from Sicily, and there were many dogfights. One morning our squadron was scrambled to intercept a large number of bombers escorted by fighters who were, by the time we got airborne, almost over Malta. Unusually, the island was covered by white cloud cover and we were able to see the bombers clearly. The first section of our fighters dived down and engaged the bombers while we, the second section of four, were just about to follow, when we were attacked by Italian fighters and Me 109s. A running dogfight started. In a split second the sky was filled with weaving and turning aircraft. I managed to get on the tail of an Italian Reggiane but at first could not fix my gun sights on him as he violently manoeuvred to avoid me. As he broke to dive and turn for home I did manage to let fly a quick burst of cannon shells and may have damaged him, but did not claim [a kill].

A new tactic by the *Luftwaffe* emerged whereby a squadron of Italian fighters would fly with the bombers at 20,000ft while the Me 109 escorts would be above them at 30,000ft. The scrambled Spitfires would of course engage the escorting Italian fighters in order to get to the bombers. Less experienced pilots concentrating on a target would not see the Me 109s diving out of the sun to come in behind them, with deadly results. Needless to say our losses were grim and other tactics became necessary to protect the few aircraft that remained with us.

With such losses it was normal for the squadron to be heavily outnumbered by the Me 109s, usually by about five to one, but on occasions when only four of the squadron engaged it could be as high as twenty to one. My experience taught me that the Germans were immaculately disciplined and would go through hell or high water to follow an order from their leader, but they did have to have leadership. German courage was never in question; nor was the British, but ours was very different. Being an island race, it seemed to me that perhaps every man was prepared to be a leader if the circumstances dictated it. This was highlighted when engaging the bombers, we would target the leading box to destroy its leader. If this was successful the whole formation, lost without orders, could suddenly turn about or end up in such disarray they were much easier to shoot down.

Dogfights often ensued when we were bounced by the escorting Me 109s but our squadron strategy now, with aircraft so short, was to dive down on the bombers, destroy what we could and then drop back to sea level to get back to Malta without loss. We could not afford to lose a single machine. However, the Me 109s soon got wise to this and would follow us down, with the inevitable dogfight ensuing. I was caught twice this way. On the first occasion I had shot down a Ju 88 and dived down to sea level to return to base. By this time our trick of making ourselves out to be four squadrons had been picked up by the German Y service and passed onto them. Unfortunately two Me 109s spotted me and dived down to attack. I saw them coming and out-turned them. A dogfight followed. Making tight turns, I managed to sit on the tail of one and bagged him – he went into the sea. The other one was by this time getting short of fuel and turned for Sicily so I was clear to return to Malta.

# AUGUST 1942

**2 August 1942**

Log Book – Spitfire Scramble – 14+ bombers turned back. Fighters came in high and went out without contact.

Log Book – Spitfire Scramble – 15+ climbed into sun and started to jump Me 109s – they saw us unfortunately.

**5 August 1942**

Log Book – Spitfire Scramble – Water-babies patrol, four Me 109s tried to bounce us but my No. 4 shot one down, the Staffel Leader. Hell of a flap in Sicily. My No. 4 inexperienced, boy did we laugh!

An estimated twenty Me 109s in two formations approached the coast just before 9 a.m. and were met by eight Spitfires from 1435 Squadron. Blue section led by Mejor engaged them and Flight Sergeant John Pinney, a Canadian, managed to shoot one down as they were patrolling over a Catalina flying boat in Kalafrana Bay to prevent it being strafed. Pinney reported:

My section was flying along in a south-easterly direction when we were attacked by four Me 109s which broke off their attack without firing and passed over our heads, splitting into pairs. I turned and saw another pair of Me 109s diving down towards us in a south-easterly direction and completed my turn. I fired a short burst from head-on position, breaking off the attack at less than 50 yards without observing strikes. On turning again, however, I saw a Me 109 with glycol pouring from it. This aircraft has been confirmed as destroyed.

**9 August 1942**

Log Book – Spitfire Scramble – Me 109 Fighter Sweep 30,000ft. bombers turned back.

# 5

# Operation Pedestal

## THE BUILD-UP TO OPERATION PEDESTAL

Much of the island was in ruins. It had been bombed incessantly and the Maltese and all military personnel were close to starving. The bread ration had been cut again and at the beginning of July pasteurised milk was restricted to hospitals and children. Farmers had been ordered to hand over their crops to the Maltese Government and supplies of potatoes – their staple diet with bread – were now also exceedingly short. Lord Gort, the island's Governor, wrote to Prime Minister Churchill, 'Nations at war have managed to ration either bread or potatoes, but not both. To be told you will not starve, but to become conscious at the same time that your stomach is an aching void, is apt to leave the average person discontented.'

Despite all this, morale remained good, but when the Chief of the Imperial General Staff (CIGS) General Alan Brooke visited Gort on the way to Cairo to assess the position for himself and to brief Gort on future strategy, he was appalled to see grubby children with no shoes, few clothes and clearly starving as he had driven past on his way to see Gort. He noted in his diary that the destruction was inconceivable and reminded one of Ypres, Arras and Lens at their worst during the last war. Brooke also noted that the arrival of Air Vice Marshal Keith Park in July to replace Sir Hugh Pugh Lloyd had brought a fresh approach to the use of the Spitfires in an offensive rather than a defensive role on the island. With plenty of Spitfires available, the new AOC thought it made much more sense to try and intercept the enemy bombers before they reached Malta, shooting them down or breaking up their formation, a plan in theory that could save lives, time, aircraft and labour. The island's radar system was by now working much better and by insisting on a much quicker take-off time of 2 or 3 minutes and working with up to three squadrons at a time, this met with favour from the pilots. Park had also insisted that the Air Sea Rescue was improved.

Brooke spoke at length to Lord Gort, AOC Park and Vice Admiral Leatham. The target date for surrender had been put back to September thanks to the efforts in getting the small convoy through in June, but Brooke accepted that for Gort it remained a juggling exercise to manage the island's meagre stocks and also noted there appeared to be a difference of opinion between Gort and Park. Gort favoured conserving fuel, which to him meant concentrating on defending the island. Park, on the other hand, had already shown his hand and believed it was important to build up Malta's offensive capability and attack the bomber formations before they reached the island, as well as the Axis shipping and supply lines to Rommel in North Africa, which had also reached a critical stage. There, the British Eighth Army had fallen back to El Alamein. Tobruk had fallen, giving Rommel a port, but this was still over 300 miles away from the front line so Rommel's supply lines were vulnerable; and although he knew it, so did the RAF. The best way for Malta to help, in Park's view, was to continue with Malta-based aircraft attacking Rommel's convoys. To do this and to avoid the island starving, they needed more food and fuel. It was imperative that another convoy got through, and a much larger one, and there were really only two opportunities to do this, the middle of July or August when the moon was at its smallest and there would be more protective darkness. Since there had not been time to organise it for July, it had to be August. It was the narrowest of windows.

The planning for Operation Pedestal, as it was code-named, had begun in the middle of July. It was to be the largest ever convoy to Malta and the most heavily escorted Allied convoy of the war. Finding suitable merchant ships was no easy task, and speed was essential. Losses of merchant ships in the North Atlantic and Mediterranean were enormous and had proved to be a considerable drain. Officers of the naval forces were brought to London to work with the First Sea Lord and his Admiralty staff to assemble the required shipping in the UK. Eventually twelve large merchantmen, all capable of up to 15 knots, were earmarked for the operation and began assembling at Glasgow, Liverpool and Bristol.

David Macfarlane was due some belated leave but knowing that an important job was in hand, and guessing that it might be another convoy to Malta, he refused to take his leave and chose to stay with the *Melbourne Star*.

All the ships were to be given the same cargoes. The vital fuel, ammunition, food, mechanical spares and medical supplies were divided between the ships so that a portion would get through even if one or more of the ships were lost. None of the merchantmen had holds capable of carrying fuel and while they could take what was available in five-gallon cans, this would just simply not be enough. It was vital therefore to have an oil tanker. The problem was the British merchant fleet no longer had one left of sufficient size or capable of sufficient speed. Only the Americans had them and they were required by the Americans, who had now entered the war. Although there had been considerable opposition when the original request was made, the US Maritime Commission had allowed the use of two such tankers by the British. The first, the *Kentucky*, had already been sunk with the attempted June convoy; the second, the *Ohio*, was made available and on this tanker and its fuel, Malta depended. For the run to Malta, *Ohio* received a new paint job of battleship grey and her existing 5in low-angle gun and a 3in anti-aircraft gun were supplemented by six 20mm Oerlikon cannons, two Browning machine guns, one Bofors on the poop deck and four sets of parachute and cable rocket launchers.

In command of the naval forces that would escort the convoy as far as the Skerki Bank was Vice Admiral Neville Syfret. The convoy was to be protected by the largest naval defence force ever put together, and would be split into two groups, one as distant cover – known as Force Z – and the other as close support all the way to Malta – Force X. Between the two groups or forces there were assembled two battleships – *Nelson* and *Rodney* – four aircraft carriers – *Eagle*, *Victorious*, *Indomitable* and *Furious*, one of which, *Furious*, was to launch thirty-seven Spitfires to reinforce the Malta squadrons – seven light cruisers, thirty-two destroyers and five corvettes. They would separate at the entrance to the Skerki Channel, with Force Z ( the battleships, aircraft carriers and three cruisers) returning to Gibraltar, leaving just four cruisers and the destroyer flotilla as Force X to continue to escort the convoy the remaining 150 or so miles to Malta.

Loading of the ships began in earnest at Avonmouth, Bristol, Liverpool and the Clyde. Despite the supposed secrecy of the convoy, it was alarming to some who witnessed the loading that some of the crates and carboys being loaded were stamped with 'Malta'. Torpedoes, high-octane fuel, machine guns and ammunition provided a volatile and deadly cargo.

Macfarlane recorded:

In the early hours of Saturday morning 1 August 1942 we left our berth at King George V Dock to go to our appointed anchorage off Gourock, but before anchoring we proceeded to calibrate the DF [Direction Finder], test the DG ['degaussing', the process of decreasing or eliminating a magnetic field] and then adjust the compasses. On Sunday 2 August the balance of the oil fuel cargo was taken on board. In the afternoon the First Wireless Operator and I went ashore to attend a conference at Gourock, after which we were taken on board HMS *Nigeria* for another conference – this the most important. Here we were given our final orders and were informed that Malta was our final destination. The secrecy of our mission was impressed upon us all and after our conference was over we were not allowed to get in touch or communicate in any way with anyone ashore. We were conveyed back to our respective ships by launch.

Those ships on the Clyde left on 2 August and were joined by their escorts the following morning. Just prior to sailing, but after the preliminary convoy conference, Rear Admiral Burrough met with the Convoy Commodore and the masters of the merchant ships on board his flagship, HMS *Nigeria*, and the whole plan for the convoy was explained in detail. A similar meeting with all the radio operators of the merchant ships to explain fleet communications and radio transmission (RT) procedures was also completed, and personal messages signed by the First Lord of the Admiralty wishing all the masters 'God Speed', contained in envelopes marked 'Not to be opened until 0800 hours August 10', were handed to all the ships' masters, including Macfarlane.

He recorded:

> That evening we weighed anchor and proceeded to sea in single line ahead and when clear of narrow waters formed into four columns. After several days of passage we were located by enemy reconnaissance aircraft and they shadowed us on and off for the next few days until they were certain that the convoy was bound into the Mediterranean. Several of our escort ships including HMS *Nelson* and HMS *Rodney* opened fire but to the best of my knowledge no hits were scored.

The passage of the convoy from the UK to rendezvous with the aircraft carriers and escorts west of the Straits of Gibraltar was successful but not without its alarms, as U-boat contacts were made en route and a Coastal Command Sunderland flying boat was shot down by friendly fire and nervous gunners. Despite this, the convoy had practised anti-aircraft gunnery, emergency turns and changing position within the convoy using both signal flags and short-range RT. The risk to security of breaking RT silence was accepted as a result of these exercises but the risk deemed acceptable. By Sunday 9 August the entire convoy had assembled and, before turning towards the Mediterranean, a final exercise was carried out with the whole fleet practising emergency turns and responding to simulated air attacks. If there had been any doubt in anyone's mind where they were going and how dangerous their mission was going to be, there was none now. On the night of 9–10 August they sailed past the narrows of Gibraltar; the whole fleet was blacked out but Gibraltar was ablaze with lights as usual, providing a stark contrast.

## 10 AUGUST 1942

The convoy and its escort finally sailed past Gibraltar at dawn on 10 August. On board the aircraft carrier *Furious* was Flight Lieutenant Geoffrey Wellum, one of the more experienced pilots, who would lead one of the flights to Malta. He recalled:

> There are about forty fighter pilots involved in this obviously very important operation, and of these forty, four are flight lieutenants; Eric 'Timber' Woods, a delightful Scotsman called Magruder, another named Bill Rolls and myself. In charge is Group Captain Walter Churchill, whom I met at Debden when he was due to take a Wing of Hurricanes to Russia. A highly decorated fighter pilot in his own right, he is a splendid leader and a very charming person.

The loaded Spitfires were brought up onto the flight deck to have their engines run and the new airscrews checked, together with the fuel flow from the overload tanks which had been prone to technical problems. All was hustle and bustle but still seemed fairly well organised.

Wellum was allocated Spitfire EP465 and made a point of going down to the hangar to check his aircraft over, place his parachute and make the cockpit ready for the morning. All the other pilots appeared to be doing the same thing. Whilst checking over the aircraft, an RAF armourer turned up and proceeded to take all the ammunition out of the ammunition boxes. Wellum was perplexed and a little curious. Apparently it was all about cigarettes and the weight. The armourer went on to explain that they were short of cigarettes on Malta and to make sure of the take-off weight it had been decided to take out the ammunition.

Group Captain Walter Churchill was not far away, and asked, 'Everything all right Geoffrey?' 'Yes thank you, sir,' he replied. 'I'm still learning. As you can see, I'm watching my guns being loaded with cigarettes.' 'Bloody marvellous isn't it?' said Churchill. 'I agreed to have the ammunition removed to save the weight. The fags don't weigh very much and things have been pretty tough on Malta. It will do the troops' morale a power of good to get some cheap smokes.' 'So cigarettes are the order of the day?' asked Wellum. 'Well yes, that's about the size of it'. 'That's very kind and considerate of us sir. I hope the Germans and Italians don't know.' 'What if they do – you could not hit them even with ammunition Geoffrey!' 'I know you to be right sir, but it would still be nice to be in a position to try!'

A note had been made of the aircraft numbers and what position they would occupy when coming up from the hangar to the flight deck. They had decided that as they could only get eight Spitfires off in one batch, they would have four sections of eight and one of seven as they now only had thirty-nine Spitfires on board, having sent one off on the first day to test the take-off run. The route they were to fly was over the Mediterranean to Skerki Bank, north-west of Tunis, turn south-east and then fly north of Pantelleria towards Malta. From any point north of Tunis they could expect the enemy to intercept them as they had the capability to strike from Tunis, Pantelleria and Sicily. The height would depend on cloud base and each leader would make his own decision as to the best way to get to Malta, as much would depend on what happened along the way. In the event of attack, the RT could be used but otherwise RT silence was to be maintained as they could not afford to give away their positions to the Germans.

# 11 AUGUST 1942

Approaching midday on 11 August it was planned to despatch thirty-eight Spitfires (one of the original thirty-nine had become unserviceable) from HMS *Furious* as part of Operation Bellows in three flights of eight and two flights of seven. Group Captain Churchill and Wing Commander A.H. Donaldson would lead the first two flights, Wellum the third flight, and Pilot Officer W.T. Rolls and Flight Lieutenant E.P. Magruder the next two flights.

The first two Spitfire flights got away en route to Takali. As Wellum was checking his Spitfire ready for him to lead the third flight, there were four enormous crumps and brown puffs of smoke seen rising from HMS *Eagle* a mile to the starboard side. 'Christ – what was that?' thought Wellum. Something had obviously happened to the *Eagle* – he thought she had been torpedoed. Now she had stopped, smoke was pouring from her and she started to list to port. She was sinking rapidly. Planes could be seen slipping off the flight deck and men were jumping into the sea. Destroyers were dashing about and depth charges going off looking for the submarine responsible. It was chaos.

Captain L.D. Mackintosh DSC on board HMS *Eagle* had positioned the carrier well over on the starboard quarter of the convoy whilst HMS *Charybdis* kept close station on her. She was steaming at 13 knots with four Sea Hurricanes aloft on patrol, sharing the duty with four from HMS *Victorious*. At 1.15 p.m. observers saw four explosions along her port side and she immediately began to list to port.

The first torpedo had struck the *Eagle*'s port quarter and was followed 10 seconds later by three more. All hit between her P2 and P3 6in guns. After the first strike she heeled over 5 degrees to port and this increased to 15 degrees with the final strike, with all the explosions in the vicinity of the port wing engine room. Boiler rooms A, C and D were quickly flooded and the port wing bulkhead collapsed. She sank within 6 minutes.

On board *Eagle* there was a mix of panic and a total misunderstanding or appreciation of what had happened. One survivor recalled:

It was when we dropped astern of the convoy to take on returning aircraft (the patrolling Sea Hurricanes) that we got hit amidships by four torpedoes. I cannot remember hearing the order to abandon ship but it was obvious as she immediately started to go down on the port side, the aircraft began sliding overboard and a lot of the ship's company too, including one of my close shipmates, never to be seen again. I think from the time she was hit she was gone in seven minutes. The ship was at action stations and my station was on the forward multiple pom-pom. Before going over the side I tried to close the ammunition locker to stop shells coming out and hitting people on the flight deck. When I thought it was time to go I walked down the ship's side on to the bilges with a lot more of the ship's company, blew up my lifebelt and jumped in. At first I was drawn down by the suction of the ship sinking, but then came to the surface and managed to grab a mess deck stool floating by with about six others. We got fairly shook up by the depth charges from the destroyers looking for the submarine. After some time, it seemed like hours, we were picked up by a boat lowered by the tug *Jaunty* and from there transferred to a destroyer, HMS *Malcolm*, which returned us to Gibraltar.

A member of 824 Squadron aboard *Eagle* also recalled the tragic events:

I was on duty on the flight deck when there [were] four large explosions on the port side and the ship listed over immediately. Because we had been bombed so many times previously I thought it was yet another air attack, but as the ship failed to come upright again I knew it was no bombing. In no time the flight deck was under water on the port side and the aircraft were sliding into the water. I managed to get to the edge of the flight deck and scramble down the drop into the sea. I was a reasonable swimmer and managed to get away as far as I could. On looking back I could see the ship upside down and sinking fast, with many people on the upturned bottom of the ship as she went down. They can only have been non-swimmers, as the biggest hazard was the non-swimmers asking for help. After what seemed an age I was picked up by the destroyer HMS *Laforey* and transferred to HMS *Keppel*.

HMS *Laforey* and the tug *Jaunty* were ordered to pick up survivors. Although *Eagle* sank quickly in approximately 6 minutes, the quick actions of these ships rescued 67 officers and 862 ratings from the ship's complement of 1,160.

Another rating on board **HMS** *Eagle* recalled:

I was standing in the shade of No.1 starboard 6in gun, 50ft above the waterline. The *Eagle* shuddered with four distinct lurches. For some reason I thought we had hit a school of whales! The deck tilted under my feet and to my astonishment I saw a pair of sea boots flying through the air and disappear overboard. These were followed by other pieces of debris and as the ship began to list I realised that we were in serious trouble.

Loose fittings began to clatter around. Frightened voices shouted and men began to stream up from the lower decks to reach higher positions. Bodies were already floundering in the water below. The wake of the *Eagle* had developed a distinct curve as the vessel pulled out of line. The rhythmic throb of the main engines died away and the ship slewed further around, rapidly keeling over.

Looking over the side I was amazed to see that the green-slimed bulge of the torpedo blister was above the surface of the water. (Designed to withstand a charge of 750lb per square inch, the torpedo blister was supposed to deflect the force of underwater explosions and preserve the hull of the ship.)

I never did hear the order to abandon ship, but when I saw Marines jumping from the flight deck, hurtling past the gun deck and hitting the rising torpedo blister as the ship keeled over, I really did begin to get worried. Less than 2 minutes had passed, and the Marines [who] had smashed themselves to jelly when they jumped had already slithered away, leaving behind a blood-streaked trail of slime.

I clambered through the rails, and suddenly I too was sitting on the torpedo blister. Two ratings were already there, terrified; they could not swim. An officer slid between the two ratings and shouted, 'now is your time to learn', and with a rating beneath each arm he dived into the sea. I never saw them again.

Taking a deep breath, I blew up my inflatable lifebelt which was a permanent part of our dress when we were afloat. Remembering our survival lectures, I hurriedly kicked off my deck shoes, pushed myself away and before I could think I was upside down 20ft under the water and frantically holding my breath whilst I looked around for a lighter colour in my surroundings that would indicate the surface. The next few seconds seemed like a lifetime and as I broke through to the surface my throat and chest seemed to explode with relief.

When I was able to think, I heard someone shouting, 'Get the charges'. 'Oh my God!' I thought. The depth charges for the air-craft, were they primed? My horizon from wave level was limited. *Eagle* was just a bulge in my vision. Then she was gone. My throat filled with bile, and as I looked around my small watery world I saw other frightened faces and suddenly I did not feel quite so lonely. 'Swim away from the ship, depth charges, suction, the boilers will explode!' All these things went through my brain, but where was the ship? Which was the way to swim? Swim! Swim! Swim! The sea suddenly boiled; an unbelievable crushing pressure stunned my senses, and I spun around in the water like a toy and when I could think again I was once more in my own little watery world. Something bumped into me from behind; it was 'Stripey', the 12-year service man who was the 'Daddy' of our mess deck, but something was wrong. His face was discoloured, his eyes staring, and he was flopping uncontrollably in the water. I grabbed for him, and my clutch slithered down his torso, and suddenly there was nothing but mush.

From the waist down he was just offal, sliced in half, and gone. Panic-stricken, I pushed him away and felt my stomach heaving uncontrollably. We drifted apart.

Apart from the Spitfires including Wellum's aboard *Furious* still waiting to get away, a pilot on board HMS *Indomitable* was also in the cockpit of his Sea Hurricane waiting to take off:

The wind was chancy and we were to be boosted off. I was in position on the catapult, engine running. The flight deck engineer waggled the ailerons to draw my attention to something or other and I looked out over the port side to see what he wanted. As I did so I stared in horror beyond him to where the *Eagle* was steaming level with us, half a mile away, with smoke and steam pouring from her. She quickly took on a heavy list and the air shook with a series of muffled explosions. There had hardly been time to assimilate the fact that she had been hit before she had capsized and sank. When I took off a few minutes later I was still numbed by what I had seen. It had come so completely without warning.

Macfarlane, on board the *Melbourne Star*, reported:

Nothing of note happened until a few minutes after 1 p.m. on Tuesday 11 August when three or four explosions were felt, and on looking westwards, I saw the aircraft carrier *Eagle* heeling over badly, the planes were slipping off her decks into the sea. I also saw what appeared to me to be an attempt by a pilot to take his plane off the ship but he was unable to do so, which was perhaps just as well, as if he had succeeded I think he would have swept many men into the sea. The *Eagle* sank in less than 10 minutes.

Captain Roger Hill on board HMS *Ledbury* also saw what had happened:

At about 13.00 when I was sitting in my high chair on the bridge I suddenly felt several heavy shocks through the hull of the ship, then the sound of explosions and a cry – it's the *Eagle*. Looking astern I saw a great column of dark-coloured smoke drifting from the port side of the carrier. She had been flying off planes and was going at full speed and was already beginning to list. HMS *Derwent* made a signal to me 'Pick up survivors' which I thought damn silly since I was one of the destroyers detailed for the final run to Malta and had little spare fuel. I queried the signal but it was repeated so round I went. The *Eagle* had been torpedoed by a German U-boat which had got through the screen and hit her on the port side with four torpedoes. She just went on listing to port until she was on her side in the water, still going ahead, and drove herself under. It was a terrible sight to see such a big ship go down so quickly. The great patch of oil and debris was full of heads, there were hundreds swimming and choking in the water.

It was vital to get the rest of the Spitfires from HMS *Furious* away, as there were obviously submarines about. Drill kicked in on board the *Furious*. The flight deck officers gave the start-up signal to the leading aircraft, keen to get them away in view of what had happened to the *Eagle*. *Furious* slowly turned into wind and worked up to full speed of 35 knots. Engines were running, pilots checked their brakes were on and in turn they waved away the chocks. The drill on the flight deck and with the deck officers was exemplary. Relaxed, or so he thought, in the cockpit of the Spitfire, Wellum recalled he could feel the aeroplane and was ready to go when given the word. He checked the airscrew control was in fine pitch again and thought that the flight deck seemed bloody short from where he was sat but this was not the time to put a spanner in the works by making a balls-up of the start! He kept an eye on the flight deck officer, who raised both his arms above his head; in his right hand was a green flag, with his left he gave the thumbs up, and then rotated his flag, to which Wellum returned the thumbs up and slowly opened the throttle. The green flag was rotated quicker, he gave the Spitfire more throttle and it wanted to go against the brakes. With that, the flag fell, Wellum applied full throttle, all he had with 3,000rpm, and he was away. Keeping the plane straight, he accelerated down the deck towards the ramp, straight down the centre line, hit the ramp and he was up, thrown into the air, literally, and away, building up speed as he put the undercarriage up and started to climb away. He remembered to put the flaps down, to lose the wooden blocks, and the flaps back up to resume normal flight. He set course for Cap Bon and Malta.

Below him, the rest of his flight was still taking off with *Furious* still maintaining full speed and leaving a white wake stretching far behind her. The flight formed on him and then *Furious* broke RT silence and warned everyone to keep clear of the carrier because of imminent air attack. Wellum did as instructed, kept clear and steadily climbed away, leaving the convoy behind. A huge flak barrage was put up against the attacking enemy aircraft.

Pilot Officer W.T. 'Bill' Rolls was due to lead the final flight of Spitfires away from *Furious* but he was on the bridge when the siren sounded, and the convoy had come under attack. He had seen the explosions on the *Eagle* and its subsequent sinking.

It was a terrible sight with all those men in the water and the destroyers racing about trying to sink the submarine that had got her. Captain T.O. Bulteel on the *Furious* decided to restart operations to launch the rest of the Spitfires and the next batch of eight was brought up on deck just before 2 p.m. Rolls was preparing himself for the take-off when he overheard naval officers discussing the proposed launch of the final flights of Spitfires. It was what he heard that worried him – their view was:

> they would not want to be in the next batch away, they don't stand an earthly chance of getting to Malta, Jerry will know by reports of this batch going off in a few minutes that operations have restarted and by now will have his aircraft waiting. If Jerry doesn't get the first lot, he is bound to get the next batch.

In reply, 'fancy all that way on one engine and if anything happens you are either drowned or blown to pieces. I feel sorry for the poor bastards.'

He did not say anything about the overheard conversation, went down to the hangar to make sure his section were getting ready for take-off, once the next batch which were now lined up on the deck had got away. He went back up on deck to watch the take-off. Three got away safely but the fourth hit the ramp, swerved back into the bridge and folded up. Within seconds the deck crews were pulling the unfortunate pilot from the Spitfire, and it was tossed over the side. The rest were then able to take off and join their leader who was circling round waiting for them.

Rolls had decided by then that he would not follow the same route to Malta that the other flights had taken. He was going to fly over Cape Bougaroni, then south of Tunis and over Hammamet, and from there he would change course to take them over Pantelleria and a direct course about 5 miles south-west of Malta. By diving down to sea level at Hammamet he hoped the German radar would not pick them up and even if they did, it would not be clear where they were heading. For all they thought it could well have been North Africa.

Rolls had taken off and was waiting for the other aircraft in his flight to join him when he realised that one of his charges was in trouble. It appeared that one of the pilots had jettisoned his long-range tank, without which he could not make Malta. In fact Sergeant Pilot Allen Stead from the RNZAF (Royal New Zealand Air Force) had discovered that his long-range tank was not feeding through correctly. They had been told that if they experienced problems immediately after take-off they were to bail out near a destroyer, which would pick them up. This had been greeted with derision as the pilots knew the navy would not want to pick up stragglers if U-boats were about, so Stead decided to attempt to land on the nearest available aircraft carrier, in his case HMS *Indomitable*. Given that none of them had been trained for such an event, this was brave, foolhardy or both. After a low pass where he came in too fast, he successfully managed to land at the second attempt, to his huge relief.

With the Spitfires successfully launched from HMS *Furious* and her part of Operation Bellows completed, she turned back towards Gibraltar with her destroyer escort sent out to get her back in safely. *Furious* went straight into dock to load a further twenty-three Spitfires for Malta, which she would fly off on 17 August.

Bill Rolls thought his change of course for Malta put his pilots in a better frame of mind, but it would also confuse Jerry. He remarked that they all looked so bloody happy every time he looked at them and his leadership was rewarded with a tight formation and an uneventful passage to Malta. After almost 3 hours and Malta about 50 miles away, the cloud started to thicken up and visibility was poor. He did not want to mess things up and miss the island. He took the flight to 8,000ft, called Malta and descended through cloud. He heard a calm voice answering the RT call sign, telling him to vector north-east for 8 miles and land at Luqa. He was a very relieved man.

Geoffrey Wellum was also a relieved and satisfied man. He too had managed to get his formation of nine Spitfires to Malta, 'Everything goes according to plan, Linosa is where it should be and I let down slowly to 15,000ft, and looking out to my right I can faintly discern the shape of Lampedusa. Last lap Geoff, nearly there, just keep steady as you go.'

Not long after, their destination appeared, looking like a brown leaf floating on water. As they approached they could see no signs of dust so there did not appear to be an air raid on:

Dropping down to 10,000ft Wellum called Malta on the RT, getting an immediate response:

We are now under the control of Malta and they say that the island is clear of enemy activity. I can now relax and merely follow their instructions. As my wheels touch down safely on Luqa, I can't help but feel a sense of satisfaction as I have helped to deliver a formation of nine Spitfires to Malta intact and in good order. At the end of my landing run a Jeep is waiting, out of which descend a crowd of RAF people. The driver of the Jeep beckons me to follow him and he guides me to a blast pen where a crowd of airmen and soldiers are waiting. Glancing behind, I see that all the others have a chap sitting on their wing guiding them into similar blast pens, where ground crew also wait. They appear organised and on the ball here, so even before I've had time to switch off and the airscrew has stopped, a mass of bodies swarm all over my Spitfire, clambering on the wings, unloading the cigarettes and replacing them with cannon shells and bullets, and the soldiers are helping refuel with 5 gallon petrol tins. Getting out of my cockpit I jump to the ground and stretch; it's good to be able to walk around and I'm not sorry that little escapade is over.

With all the fighting away to the west and apart from the arrival of the Spitfires, Malta experienced a relatively uneventful day. 1435 Squadron was scrambled twice but only once did any of them open fire. The squadron was boosted by the arrival of Wing Commander Pete 'Prosser' Hanks and Wellum from those flown in from *Furious*. Hanks led the squadron on both occasions.

John Mejor recorded 'Scramble Spitfire Vb – Fighter Sweep Angels 30' but he makes no mention of the incoming pilots or the convoy at this stage.

Later that evening, Axis aircraft caught up with the convoy but although there were a number of near misses, no other ship was sunk that day and all the while they were inching closer to the Sicilian Narrows.

On board MV *Melbourne Star*, Macfarlane reported:

Late in the afternoon of the 11th the first air attacks commenced and continued until after dark. After darkness had set in, I saw several of what appeared to be our planes returning from chasing the enemy, they could not land on our carriers, so the pilots had to bale out and crash their planes, the pilots being picked up by destroyer escorts. All quiet throughout the night.

Meanwhile at Luqa, the work of re-arming and re-fuelling the Spitfires from HMS *Furious* went on without pause. Wellum records:

I am in the act of taking off my parachute when an open MG pulls up, behind the wheel is Air Marshall Keith Park who is now AOC Malta. Following up is the Jeep that led my Spitfire to the dispersal pen, in the Jeep, Wing Commander 'Prosser' Hanks. I have never met him before but I know of him. He is a well-known fighter pilot having been with No. 1 Squadron in France before the evacuation at Dunkirk. With him is Squadron Leader Stan Grant, another Battle of Britain pilot. At that time he was with 65 Squadron, so although I don't know him well, we have something in common. As all the pilots who flew from HMS *Furious* are experienced it would appear there is a pretty strong team building on Malta.

AOC Park recognised Wellum from the Battle of Britain. 'Have we met?' Park asks. 'Yes sir, Biggin Hill, September 1940,' Wellum replies. 'Of course, I remember faces. What Squadron?' '92 sir.' 'Splendid, good to have you here. Did you take off before *Eagle* was sunk?' 'No sir, we were sitting in our cockpits when she was hit.' 'Well I don't want the word getting round just yet to the Maltese if it can be avoided. Their morale has taken enough knocks for the moment and we don't want to make things worse.' 'Understood sir.'

Wellum now knew he was joining 1435 Squadron. The other flight commander was Basil Friendship, whom Wellum got on well with from his time at Aston Down Officer Training Unit (OTU). Their CO was to be Squadron Leader Tony Lovell, who he has not met before. Quietly spoken, Lovell was very correct in every-thing he did and even after a day at dispersal and in all the dust and heat, his appearance was one of tidiness and neatness. There was nothing dishevelled or ruffled about Lovell, no matter what.

Lovell briefed the arriving pilots. Every Spitfire that had been on Malta had been flown in, so with this new batch, he informed them, they also had an adequate stock of pilots so his intention was to start a routine of one day on duty, one day off duty. Most of the aircraft losses were on the ground, bombed as a result of the Germans seeing them arrive on their radar.

## 12 AUGUST 1942

By the morning of 12 August the convoy was south of Sardinia and north of Tunisia, within easy reach of a whole host of Axis airfields and a concentration of enemy submarines. From this point on they could expect round the clock attention from every aircraft the enemy could send from Sicily and Sardinia, and by noon the bombers could rely on fighter escorts. To aid them it was another gloriously sunny day with a smooth calm sea and near perfect visibility.

The two remaining carriers flew off standing patrols of Fulmars and Sea Hurricanes, two from each ship at first light, and later a standing patrol of twelve fighters was constantly airborne with all other planes at instant readiness. But the fighters did not have the speed to intercept the German reconnaissance planes, and despite their vigilance the convoy was never completely clear of enemy aircraft.

Macfarlane recalled:

Quietness then reigned until daylight on Wednesday the 12th, when air attacks again commenced and continued throughout the day. At about midday the SS *Deucalion* was damaged by bombs and had to reduce speed to about 10 knots; she was left behind with a destroyer escort to make her own way to Malta.

The first attack came in from twenty Ju 88s just after 9 a.m. and the convoy's Sea Hurricanes, Fulmars and Martlets were scrambled to meet the more powerful German bombers. The lack of speed from the British fighters did not deter them and four Ju 88s were claimed shot down, some bombers jettisoned their bombs, but the rest carried on with their attack, screaming in on shallow dive-bombing runs out of the sun. The barrage of anti-aircraft fire put up was intense and two more bombers were claimed as destroyed. Pilots returned to the aircraft carriers full of claims and wild exaggerations, in the confusion perhaps understandable, but nevertheless they had put up a good show. Later, a couple of reconnaissance shadow aircraft were dispatched by the Fulmars until there was a lull before the main attack came in around midday. First came Italian dive bombers (thirty-three Savoia-Marchetti (SM) 79s and ten SM 84s) escorted by fighters (twenty-six Re 2001s) from their Sardinian airfields, followed up by thirty-seven Ju 88s at higher altitude. The Italians had combined all available forms of attack into one combined assault designed to cause maximum damage and confusion, and hoped to be able to make the convoy scatter and take avoiding action, enabling their new weapon, circling mines, to be launched from their torpedo bombers. This new type of mine would be dropped by parachute ahead of any target, and when it hit the water an automatic pressure device activated a propeller which drove the mine around in a circle with a radius of up to 15km.

The first waves arrived over the convoy, but instead of attacking together to cause maximum confusion, some waves were slightly delayed. The circling mines were dropped but the convoy managed to avoid them by making an emergency turn 45 degrees to port and back again to starboard. Despite the disjointed attacks, the Italians pressed home as best they could but no damage was caused and the Italians lost one SM 79, two SM 84s and an escorting Re 2001 fighter, with many others damaged by the intense flak barrage put up by the convoy and its protecting fighters.

About twelve of the Ju 88s penetrated the barrage put up by the destroyers and the fighters flown off the carriers to intercept them. The *Deucalion* was the first merchant ship to be hit; the leading freighter of the port wing column was straddled by a four-bomb stick from one of Ju 88s, three were near misses but the fourth bomb hit and seriously disabled her. HMS *Bramham* was sent to her rescue and picked up those of her crew who had abandoned ship, thinking she was sinking. In fact the engine room was not flooded, the engines were restarted and she was able to make headway at around 8 knots. At this speed it was impossible for her to catch up with the rest of the convoy, which maintained about twice that speed, so with HMS *Bramham* as escort they were told to use an inshore route closer to the Tunisian coast. They were found again at around 8 p.m. when two Ju 88s swooped in low, but the fire from the *Bramham* meant that both bombers missed their target. They were not so fortunate about an hour later when two Heinkel (He) 111 bombers attacked with their engines cut, out of the sun, and hit *Deucalion* with two torpedoes. Mortally hit this time, HMS *Bramham* picked up survivors and made off, watching her sink lower in the water until a loud explosion finished her off and she sank with her precious cargo.

Meanwhile, back with the main convoy and after the attacks just after lunch had been beaten away, two Italian Re 2001 fighters joined returning Sea Hurricanes in the circuit to come into land on HMS *Victorious*. They achieved complete surprise when they broke away from the Hurricanes and dropped their bombs on the flight deck – fortunately it was armoured and the 100lb bombs caused little damage, although four officers and two men were killed as one of the bombs showered the flight deck with splinters as it exploded.

With these air attacks over, the submarines closed in and Anti-Submarine Detection (ASDIC) soundings continued throughout the afternoon. One Italian submarine was badly damaged by the destroyer escort dropping depth charges, and was driven down to a depth that made her crew's nose and ears bleed. As she fought to regain control she was over-trimmed and broke surface astern of the convoy, where her conning tower was spotted by HMS *Ithuriel*. Before the unfortunate Italian submarine could dive again, she was rammed by the *Ithuriel* and sunk, though three of her officers, including the Captain, and thirty-eight crew ratings were picked up by the destroyer.

Lieutenant Commander D.H. Maitland-Makgill-Crichton DSO RN, captain of HMS *Ithuriel*, recorded:

'Stand by depth-charges. Depth-charges, fire.' The able seaman standing by the firing levers pulls them, and after a few seconds the ship shudders as they explode violently astern of us. 'Quite a good attack I think, Sir,' says the RNVR Sub-Lieutenant, and everybody looks astern, hoping for some signs of wreckage to appear.

I decide to carry out a second depth-charge attack and the ship is just turning when a roar goes up, 'There she is.' It was a successful attack, and the U-boat has come to the surface, but the job is not yet finished. Perhaps she will crash-dive and try to escape. We can take no chances. So, 'Full ahead both engines; prepare to ram.' The guns need no orders. They have already opened fire and the U-boat is getting seven bells knocked out of her.

Some of the Italians start shouting and jumping overboard. I give the order 'Full speed astern' to take some speed off the ship and avoid damaging ourselves unnecessarily. After all, you don't need to use a hammer on a boiled egg, so to speak. We hit her abaft the conning tower and heel her right over. It is a delightful crunch.

By now isolated, *Ithuriel* came under attack from four Ju 88s and escorting fighters, and with her speed reduced to around 20 knots she had to carefully steer her way through the bomb bursts before she was able to rejoin the convoy. The convoy had managed to fight off this succession of attacks from the air but was now approaching the point close to the Skerki Channel where Vice Admiral Syfret would have to give the order for the heavy escorting force to turn back towards Gibraltar. For the loss of the *Eagle* and one merchantmen, the rest of the convoy had made it nearly 800 miles and were only 300 miles from Malta – but there could be no room for complacency. The greatest dangers still lay ahead, from both further submarine and E-boat attacks in the narrow Skerki Channel and air attacks from the Sicilian airfields. Vice Admiral Syfret notified all ships that the escorting force would turn back just after 7 p.m.

It was about 6 p.m. when the next heavy air attack came in, perfectly timed and executed with great determination from forty-two Ju 88s and Ju 87s, the fearsome German-made dive bombers (though some of these were Italian crewed Ju 87s), forty Savoias and thirty-eight escorting fighters.

They singled out a second aircraft carrier, HMS *Indomitable*, for attack. Sensibly, the Germans and Italians were trying to neutralise the threat from the escorting fighters first. Peeling off between 9,000 and 10,000ft, some of the pilots came down as low as 1,000ft in attempts to hit the carrier. All the carrier's guns opened up in a desperate attempt to deter the Ju 87s. Men on board other ships in the convoy watched in horror as *Indomitable* gradually became enveloped in smoke and obscured by bomb splashes as hits on her flight deck took hold, and she circled slowly and painfully to avoid further hits. She turned away from the wind in an attempt to master the fires which swept her hangar decks. One bomb had landed near the forward lift and exploded above the main hangar deck, and a hole some 20ft by 12ft was blown in the upper deck. Severe structural and splinter damage was caused between the flight deck and the lower gallery deck. The forward lift was canted up by about 6ft and stuck. A second bomb hit the after lift, went through the upper gallery deck and exploded above the upper hangar deck, destroying the hangar with a fire breaking out near the torpedo room. Mercifully, the torpedo warheads did not explode. In addition to the two direct hits there were several near misses causing further damage, and by the time the Ju 87s had vanished the *Indomitable* was finished as a fighting unit. The carnage aboard ship was unimaginable – the wardroom had been filled with off-duty pilots and personnel from 827 Fleet Air Arm Squadron when one of the near miss bombs killed everyone there. In all, six officers and forty-four men were killed and a further fifty-nine were seriously wounded, many of them Royal Marines who had manned the port guns and had suffered terribly when both turrets had been hit.

With the flight deck out of action and the aircraft carrier no longer able to land aircraft, HMS *Indomitable*'s aircraft had to be landed on HMS *Victorious*, but several fighters had to be ditched overboard to make space for further landings. In the same attack the destroyer HMS *Foresight* was torpedoed aft and, unable to continue, was later abandoned and scuttled. The loss of *Foresight* meant the convoy only had three fast minesweeping destroyers left – HMS *Fury*, *Intrepid* and *Icarus* – to lead it through the minefields.

It had been intended that Force Z would turn back at this time and Admiral Syfret had already notified the ships that this would be bought forward slightly given that HMS *Indomitable* was on fire and HMS *Rodney* had suffered boiler trouble, but the operation to turn the bulk of the escorting ships back towards Gibraltar was completed and went unnoticed by the Axis forces.

On board *Melbourne Star*, Macfarlane recorded:

> At about 7 p.m. just before the battleships and aircraft carriers with their cruiser and destroyer escorts were due to leave us, a very heavy air attack developed in which the dive bombers concentrated on the aircraft carrier *Indomitable*, scoring direct hits on her flight decks fore and aft causing fires. It was a most impressive sight to see her anti-aircraft guns still blazing furiously out through the flames and later to see her steaming westwards towards the setting sun with the fires still burning furiously.

An hour after Force Z turned westward, at about 8 p.m., the Italian submarine *Axum*, which had been following the convoy for some time but out of reach of the destroyer screen, launched an attack and fired a salvo of four torpedoes which struck *Nigeria*, *Cairo* and the oil tanker *Ohio*. As a result of *Nigeria* being hit, Rear Admiral Burrough transferred his flag to the destroyer *Ashanti*. The effect of the attack by the Italian submarine was far-reaching

– the timing critical, for the convoy was at that moment changing its disposition from four columns to two to pass through the mine-fields and for this manoeuvre the cruisers were needed as column leaders. The torpedoing of *Nigeria* and *Cairo*, and the diversion of *Ashanti* and detachment of four Hunt-class destroyers to stand by the damaged cruisers, temporarily deprived Force X of its com-mander, prevented either column of ships from having a leader and lost the convoy nearly half its escort and the entire force its two fighter direction ships, *Nigeria* and *Cairo*. These two ships had special radar and radio communication equipment to enable the convoy to communicate with land-based RAF aircraft. With the loss of these two ships, the convoy was unable to communicate with and give directions to the RAF on Malta.

With *Cairo* so badly damaged she was abandoned and sunk by other escort ships, and *Nigeria* turned westwards to join Force Z and was later sent back to Gibraltar with the other damaged Royal Navy ships *Bicester*, *Amazon*, *Antelope*, *Wishart* and *Zetland* as escorts.

Between 8.30 p.m. and 9 p.m. the convoy was subjected to further heavy air attacks by dive bombers and torpedo bombers. *Ashanti* and *Penn* combined to provide a smokescreen in an attempt to hide the merchant ships, but this did not prevent the attack from being effective. *Empire Hope* was bombed and badly dam-aged, its crew being rescued by HMS *Penn*, which then torpedoed the stricken merchantman. At about the same time *Brisbane Star* was struck by a torpedo in the forefoot and was forced to slow down, though her crew were able to shore up the forward bulk-heads and she was able to continue but at a much reduced speed. Another victim was the *Clan Ferguson* when she was also torpedoed shortly after 9 p.m. Aviation fuel stowed on deck was ignited and ammunition in the lower hold exploded and sent flaming gaso-line everywhere. Crewmen on other ships looked on in horror as smoke and flame plumes reached nearly 2,000ft into the sky, and many thought no one could have survived such an attack. The ship sank surrounded by a sea of flames but many of the crew were able to get away in lifeboats and rafts.

Macfarlane recorded:

At about 9 p.m. when we were changing formation from four columns to two, the convoy was attacked by U-boats, torpedo bombers, high level bombers and dive bombers. HMS *Nigeria* was torpedoed and HMS *Nelson* was bombed and later had to be sunk by our own forces. The tanker *Ohio* was also torpedoed at the same time. Shortly afterwards, while we were still trying to form up into two columns, the SS *Clan Ferguson* was hit and blew up, the MV *Brisbane Star* was torpedoed and the SS *Empire Hope* was bombed, set on fire and had to be abandoned later.

We were still trying to get into formation when the SS *Port Chalmers* which was on my starboard beam suddenly decided to turn around, and to avoid a collision, I had to put my helm hard a port, increase speed and turn too. On completion of turn I signalled the SS *Port Chalmers*, which was the Commodore's ship, 'What are you doing?' and he replied 'I am going west'. For a while we thought this was an order he had received and we had not. We followed him, but shortly afterwards, after talking the matter over with my senior officers and the naval liaison officer, we decided that as we had received no orders to this effect we would turn around again and proceed to Malta. This we did and just as we were going on to our old course we received a signal on a lamp from a destroyer which was 120 degrees – this being the course we had previously been on. We soon returned to where several of the ships were blazing furiously and found most of the convoy still there but could see no escort.

As we passed close to one American ship which I think was the SS *Santa Elisa* I hailed her by megaphone and told her we were proceeding to Malta and asked her if she would follow us, and she replied 'yes'. We increased to full speed, making our way to

Cape Bon with the SS *Santa Elisa* following us and I think another ship fell into line. Just as we were approaching Cape Bon light-house we were overtaken by a destroyer, we gave her our name and asked whether we should follow her and she replied 'yes follow me'. This we proceeded to do and followed her inside the minefield (bomb alley and/or E-boat alley) until we reached the light to the southward of Cape Bon, where we came upon the disabled cruiser HMS *Manchester*. The destroyer hauled in towards the cruiser and we followed but she signalled us to carry on, which we did. A short time later she appeared out of the darkness and we attempted to follow her again but we could not keep up with her and we had also out-distanced the other two ships which were following us. I would like to state before going any further that as we proceeded inside the minefields close into the coast we saw ahead of us great activity in the way of tracer shells and bullets, which indicated that E-boat attacks were being made but fortunately by the time we arrived at the same spot all was quiet again.

After increasing speed when proceeding on our own and later we were giving a wonderful fireworks display from our exhaust, and this made us a very good target. I was very perturbed about it, however everything possible had been done to stop the display without success. We carried on after losing the destroyer, keeping well away to the southward all the time, as all activity seemed to be to the northward, and we eventually came up to a destroyer escort. It was just about at this time that we received an SOS message by wireless that the MV *Wairangi* had been torpedoed and stopped. We heard nothing more but know that she eventually sank.

We kept zigzagging to the southward of the destroyers and tried at intervals to drop in astern of one of them, but none of them seemed to want us there and we began to think we were nobody's baby and we had to keep pulling away.

# 13 AUGUST 1942

They had made it through the night, but only just. Macfarlane had manoeuvred the *Melbourne Star* into position with what remained of the convoy in single line. *Rochester Castle* was leading, followed by *Waimarama*, then the *Melbourne Star* with the *Ohio* behind him. *Port Chalmers* was some way behind and had not caught up with them.

On the bridge of the *Melbourne Star* Macfarlane peered into the darkness before first light and wondered what else could be thrown at the convoy. Only half the convoy had survived the night and daybreak would bring no relief, only more Axis bombers and, for all he knew, Italian cruisers and destroyers too. Aboard the depleted escorts and the merchant ships of the convoy, haggard and exhausted men stood ready to repel what could be the enemy's next decisive attack. Very few gave themselves much of a chance. Against everything that the Axis could launch against the remains of the convoy, there seemed little that the remaining ships could do except go down fighting.

Despite the repeated attacks, Macfarlane was aware that the damaged tanker the *Ohio* was still making decent progress. Supreme efforts were required to hold the damaged vessel on her course. Her deck had been split across the centre almost to her amidships and with every yaw of her helm the buckled metal tore and groaned, threatening to break the entire ship in half. It was necessary to keep a continuous 5 degrees on the starboard helm to compensate for the pull caused by the great gouge in her side. By 3 a.m. the tanker had managed to reach a speed of 13 knots and by dawn she had caught up with the remainder of the convoy.

They had been expecting attacks from the Italian Navy all night, and it was a miracle that there had been none. In fact the Italians had withdrawn and steamed away from the convoy because Air Vice Marshal Park, in charge of the RAF on Malta, had sent out what available aircraft he had and ordered them to illuminate the Italian cruisers and make regular reports back to Malta to convey to the Italians that a strike force of considerable size and power was on its way. This was followed up by an attack from a single Wellington and an 'illuminate and attack' call to non-existent Liberators, which resulted in the Italian Cruisers making a course for Palermo.

Good fortune, fortitude and deception had all played their part, but this did not concern Rear Admiral Burrough, who had deployed what was left of his escorts to fight a defensive action against the expected surface attack from the Italians. The force available to him was hardly impressive, however. Other than three minesweeping destroyers, he could only muster a damaged cruiser, HMS *Kenya*, and HMS *Charybdis* as heavy ships and three big Tribal-class destroyers with HMS *Pathfinder*. HMS *Bramham* was standing by the abandoned *Santa Elisa*, HMS *Penn* was coming up from astern with *Port Chalmers* while HMS *Ledbury* was close to the *Ohio* but they were about 5 miles astern of the main body which now consisted of the *Melbourne Star*, *Waimarama* and *Rochester Castle*.

Macfarlane had steered well to the south during darkness and caught up with the remaining destroyer escorts. He recalled, however, 'that they were nobody's baby, every time he steered a course to take up position astern of one of the destroyers, the escort would zigzag and pull away!' At dawn he had finally received permission to take station with one of the escorts when the *Ashanti* came up and formed alongside him on the *Melbourne Star*'s starboard side, where she hailed Macfarlane and ordered him to turn around and join the others. It turned out 'that he had been trying to form up close astern with a destroyer escort (minesweeping) that had lost its sweeps'. Macfarlane was not aware of his precarious position. The *Melbourne Star* drew far more water than the destroyer so she could not be relied upon to detonate the mines for him:

Having found a comfortable position close to an escort I was loathe to abandon it, so I shouted back to the *Ashanti* that I was quite happy where I was. Back came a stern rebuke – 'I am the Admiral' – and of course I then realised that Rear Admiral Burrough had taken station aboard the *Ashanti*!

*Melbourne Star* turned silently and rejoined the convoy, taking station astern of *Waimarama*. Thus it was that only half the convoy had survived the night, fully aware that daybreak would bring no relief. The full weight of the *Luftwaffe* and the *Regia Aeronautica* in Southern Italy and Sicily, together with the Italian cruiser and destroyer squadrons, were poised to provide the decisive final blows to the convoy.

The single line of the remnants of the convoy provided an inviting target. The ordeal of the convoy, now south-east of Pantelleria and 200 miles from Malta, began at 8 a.m. when twelve Ju 88s dived on the merchant ships. They attacked in shallow dives between 2,000 and 6,000ft with the *Ohio* attracting their main attention. She was surrounded by bomb bursts and towering walls of spray but the escorts managed to break up the attacks. Three of the bombers turned their attention to the *Waimarama*; the first missed as flak exploded around the nose of the Ju 88, but she was unable to avoid the next attack. The two Ju 88s screamed down on her and the first released a five-bomb stick that proved fatally accurate with four scoring direct hits. It was impossible for any cargo ship to survive, let alone one carrying high-octane fuel, oil and ammunition. All four hits were close together about the bridge, which disappeared as she blew up with an enormous explosion, a ball of flame enveloping the ship, followed by gigantic column of smoke through which her masts could be seen collapsing like matchsticks into the heart of the furnace. In seconds the *Waimarama* listed to starboard, righted herself and went down, leaving a huge area of flaming sea and a dense, oily cloud of smoke. The second Ju 88 was caught in the blast and disintegrated in mid-air.

Macfarlane reported:

At 8.10 a.m. during a heavy attack by torpedo and high level bombers, dive bombers suddenly came out of the sun and a stick of bombs fell on the S.S *Waimarama* which blew up and disappeared in a few seconds. We were showered with debris from the explosion and at the same time we were straddled by bombs, which fell close to the port side forward and the starboard side aft. A piece of plating 5ft long fell on board. The base of a steel ventilator, half an inch thick and 2ft 6in high, partially demolished one of our machine gun posts. At the same time a piece of angle iron narrowly missed one of the cadets. The sea was one sheet of fire and as we were so close we had to steam through it. I put the helm hard a port and had to come down from where I was on the monkey island to the bridge to save myself from being burned, and at the same time the Second Officer Mr Richards rang the telegraphs 'Full ahead' for an increase of speed. It seemed as though we had been enveloped in flame and smoke for ages, although it was only a matter of minutes, otherwise the ship could never have survived.

The flames were leaping mast-high; indeed, at times they could have reached 2,000ft with the smoke column. The heat was terrific and the air was becoming drier every minute, as the oxygen was being sucked out of it. When they inspected the damage afterwards, they found that nearly all the paint on the ship's sides had been burnt away and the bottom of the lifeboats reduced to charcoal.

Unable to see how they could avoid being blown up as they sailed through the flames, Macfarlane ordered everybody forward. However, they cleared the flames safely and he ordered everybody back to their stations. He continued:

[We] took up station astern of the SS *Rochester Castle*. Shortly afterwards it was reported to me that seventeen men were missing and later this was increased to thirty-six. All these men thinking that the forward end of the ship had been struck, and being quite certain that if they stayed aboard would be blown up, jumped over the side. All our defences had now to be reorganised. Throughout the action my men behaved splendidly, the team spirit was perfect, but after the loss of their comrades who jumped overboard, the remaining men were keener than ever and we could not hold them back.

Most of those that jumped found themselves in a worse situation in the burning sea, but many were picked up by HMS *Ledbury* and the *Ohio*. John Jackson was a radio operator on the forward bridge of the *Waimerama*, 'The ship was immediately enveloped in flames and on looking to starboard I could see nothing but a solid mass of flames. I looked across to the port side and could not even see the gun mounting which was about 2 yards away owing to the solid wall of flames.' Jackson then had to run through the bridge deckhouse, down a ladder and over debris and dead bodies, past burning and screaming men to jump into the only patch of sea that was not on fire. He wore a life vest but could not swim. There were about twenty men in the water, he recalled, who appeared to be the only survivors. 'The bridge then crumpled as it imploded, the tips of the funnels could be seen in the smoke as they collapsed and fell into the fire. Petrol cans shot into the air as they exploded and thick black smoke rose into the blue morning sky – it was hell on earth.'

Roger Hill, captain of HMS *Ledbury*, recalled the events of the early morning attack:

Torpedo planes flew in to distract attention from Ju 88s which were coming in from a height. We had detected these by RDF but could not sight them and we were slow in opening fire on them. The

*Waimarama* was hit, probably by about three or four bombs, and blew up with a tremendous explosion, leaving a great pyre of flame on the sea. HMS *Ashanti* signaled to me to pick up survivors. I went to the scene but did not think it possible that anyone could have survived such an explosion or the mass of flames, but on getting up close we could see men in the water. I cannot speak too highly of the sheer guts of these men. They were singing and encouraging each other, and as I went through them, explaining by Loudhailer that I must get the ones nearest the flames first, I received answers of 'that's alright sir, go and get the other chaps first'. The flames were spreading outward all the time, even to windward, and at one time spread the whole length of the ship while picking up two men close to the aft nets. I had to go astern, and these men were supported by my rescuers who themselves were clinging onto the nets. The last man to be picked up was on a raft which was anchored to some sunken debris in the middle of the fire. Owing to fatigue an order was repeated wrongly, and we had to go around again to get this man. I am deeply conscious that owing to this mistake I increased his suffering and his serious burns.

Another sailor who watched the terror that was the *Waimarama* unfold recalled:

The *Waimarama* blast was so intense that the crew of the *Melbourne Star* 400 yards behind, thought it was their own ship that had been hit and began jumping overboard. Mostly army gunners at the 6in and Bofors guns aft. Mad bastards they were, the gunners just disappeared overboard. It was 50 bleeding feet down to the water. No one could say we was [sic] not frightened now, we had seen too much, much too much, it was something terrible. Screaming, only screaming, terrible screaming.

# 1435 SQUADRON AIRBORNE

Everything now depended on the convoy from the west. John Mejor squinted into the rising morning sun, wondering when they would receive the order to take off. Malta's surviving Beaufighters had patrolled what was left of the convoy in the hours of darkness as it slipped through the narrow channel between the coast of Tunis and the western tip of Sicily. But the really dangerous time began now, with the dawn, as the surviving merchant ships and oil tanker, lightly escorted by destroyers, entered 'bomb alley' and the final run to the beleaguered island.

The convoy was still hours away from the island, a nightmare journey through the most bitterly contested waters in the world with the full weight of the *Luftwaffe* and *Regia Aeronautica* in southern Italy and Sicily intent on destroying what was left of it. Some time during the morning the convoy would reach a point 70 miles from Malta, when relays of Spitfires from Takali and Hal Far – every available aircraft – would endeavour to provide a continual air umbrella over the ships. Before that there was a 40-mile gap between first light and the maximum distance at which the Takali and Hal Far Spitfires could begin to provide cover. The Luqa Spitfires that had been fitted with long-range tanks would fill the gap. Only Luqa had a long enough strip of runway available to get the heavily laden fighters airborne.

Mejor looked at his watch. The squadron would be split into three sections of four aircraft and led by Wing Commander Hanks. Mejor felt a shiver run down his spine – he put it down to the aftermath of the 'Dog' attack on the contents of his stomach from which he had only recently recovered. 'Mac' – Ian Maclennan, a Canadian – had been right about the goat's milk after all, but Mejor still felt washed out and in no fit state to fly a Spitfire into action against, possibly, twenty or thirty times their number. He felt shattered.

This morning, Sykes and Tozer were his fitter and rigger, and Mejor was glad. He enjoyed the cheerful banter of the two airmen, even though he felt grim. At Luqa in these hectic days of August 1942 it was rare to get the same ground crew twice; the pilots grabbed whatever fighter was serviceable and in the months that Mejor had been on the island, he had done the rounds of just about every blast pen around the perimeter. In his mind he went over the latest situation reports. The convoy was a long way behind schedule at the last report. Suddenly he pushed himself away from the sandbags, startled by his airman's excited shout. The airman was pointing across the cratered airfield to G Shelter where a Very flare had been fired and was tracing its smoky trail through the morning haze. Sykes the fitter was already in the Spitfire cockpit and by the time Mejor got there he had the engine running. The airman relinquished his place and helped Mejor to strap himself in, dropped off the wing as Mejor taxied forward and gave him a 'thumbs up' for good luck. The other Spitfires were also emerging from their blast pens, kicking up clouds of dust as they wove their way to the runway. Mejor kept his cockpit hood open for take-off and gained a few precious seconds of cooling fresh air.

The Spitfire rumbled forward, swaying slightly as he tried to line up with the centre of the runway and opened the throttle. The tail came up reluctantly as he eased the stick forward and the speed built up agonisingly slowly as the Merlin engine coped with the extra weight of the auxiliary fuel tank. It was the same, he recalled, all those months before, when he had taken off from the USS *Wasp* to fly to Malta. This time he had slightly more runway to play with but he was almost despairing that the fighter would ever leave the ground when she bounced a couple of times and wallowed into the air, and the controls became more responsive as she steadily gained flying speed.

He pulled up the undercarriage and slammed the cockpit hood closed, turning the Spitfire quickly on the heading that ought to bring them close to the convoy, or what was left of it: 280 degrees magnetic. He formed up with the other Spitfires in formation. Radio silence was to be maintained until they were over the convoy or unless they got into trouble en route. There was no point advertising their presence or movements to the enemy. The squadron flew on steadily for several minutes. Over on the left, a lump of rock emerged from the sea, the island of Linosa. Beyond it there was nothing but a vast expanse of the open Mediterranean. They had been airborne for nearly 30 minutes and by now they should have been over the convoy. Mejor frowned and glanced at his cockpit instruments. There was nothing below him or the squadron, or anywhere in their vicinity as far as the eye could see. It occurred to him in a sudden horrifying thought that perhaps they were too late, and that the convoy had already been wiped out:

> Log Book: Spitfire VB Scramble Patrol Malta Convoy. Night take-off. Sighted Convoy 4 minutes after dawn. One ship pouring smoke.

From Malta, sections of Beaufighters were dispatched to provide the convoy with some protection, then the first flight of four Spitfires from 1435 Squadron including Johnnie Mejor arrived. The ship 'pouring smoke' was Mejor's first sight of the remnants of the convoy, just after the *Waimarama* had exploded and eighty-seven of her crew had been killed. He was not to know of the carnage unfolding beneath him. The long-range Spitfires were supposed to be operating at a maximum range of 120 miles from Malta – but they were seen over the remnants of the convoy at about 170 miles from Malta, such was their determination to get the ships through. The short-range Spitfires could take over air cover when the convoy reached 70 to 80 miles from the island.

Macfarlane reported:

We had aerial cover from Malta from the morning, Beaufighters to begin with and then Spitfires. Unfortunately we did not get the full benefit of these fighters owing to the fact that the two cruisers, HMS *Nigeria* and HMS *Cairo*, which had radio location on board, and which were meant to escort us all the way to Malta, had been sunk or damaged, and this left us without help so all the air attacks had to be sighted visually until we got close to Malta, where they could be located by the apparatus there.

Geoffrey Wellum recalled:

There was just the faintest suspicion of daylight when the first patrol heads off to cover the convoy. I watch them go, their navigation lights bright and clear as they get airborne and join up. An hour later I am taking off from Luqa with 1435 Squadron and setting course due west. On arrival where the convoy should be the haze is as thick as it was the day we flew in, and in our position the sky above is clear of enemy aircraft. To see anything below is going to be difficult with the rising sun reflecting on the haze, making it appear almost solid.

Directly below I can see a cruiser steaming at speed. She seems to be screening just two merchant ships which are pushing on independently in the general direction of Malta, and it would appear that the convoy must be pretty spread out. It has become painfully obvious that somewhere along the line they have had one hell of a battle and taken an awful pasting.

The patrol is turning out to be anything but easy and, not being used to the conditions, I find the heat through the perspex and the incessant glare troublesome. The squadron spreads out to cover as wide an area as possible. There is some faint RT in the distance. I think someone is tangling with some Ju 87s but is having problems with the haze, which of course will make the bombing difficult for the Germans. How I would love to get amongst the Ju 87s. I turn towards where I think the engagement must be but nothing comes of it. There is nothing to do but to continue patrolling, which I do. Eventually someone says he is returning to base and as my fuel is getting low I dive away with my No. 2 due east for Malta. On landing I am surprised to find that most of the squadron has returned. As I get out of my aircraft I am conscious of a horrible nagging ache around my eyes, which is disturbing. In the dispersal tent I see Tony Lovell and Basil Friendship.

As the morning wore on, one attack merged with another and one raid followed another. Later, 1435 Squadron returned and engaged the attacking Italian Stuka dive bombers, this time led by Squadron Leader Lovell. Once again the dive bombers tried in vain to attack *Ohio*, coming in steeply from several angles, timing their dives so that the ships always had several aircraft to shoot at, thus reducing the effect of the barrage put up in its defence. Despite the intensity of the attacks, the *Ohio* again came through, with one near miss by a 500lb bomb which exploded near to her bow and flooded her fore peak tanks, twisting and buckling several of her bow plates. One Stuka, hit in her dive by the combined firepower of the *Ohio* and the *Ashanti*, just disintegrated and another, although again hit, thundered into the side of the tanker after bouncing off the sea and large parts of the aircraft smashed across the tanker's poop deck, including the tail section. At about the same time a Ju 88 swept in from the port side forward at low level. A barrage of fire from the tanker and other ships nearby hit the bomber hard. It dropped into the sea, skimmed and slammed heavily into the tanker's bow, flipped over and crashed upside down on her foredeck. More Stukas roared over the tanker at mast-height and dropped a stick of bombs each side of her, and the subsequent explosions, all described as near misses, lifted the tanker clear of the water, stopping the fuel pumps and her engines. She was now stationary in the water and a sitting duck. Her crew worked wonders and managed to get the trip gear re-engaged, engines re-started and steam boosted to working pressure, so within about 20 minutes she was moving again:

Log Book: Spitfire VB Convoy Patrol – Ju 87 damaged. Control ship had been sunk. We waited up sun but the swine came in down sun. Bags of flak. We dived through and fired short bursts of one second each at three Ju 87s. Observed strikes on tail of one. I saw two Ju 88s making for the largest ship. Peeled off through flak to make head-on attack. I was hopelessly out of range but fired to scare them – it did. They dropped bombs far wide of targets and turned away. I followed. Rear gunners poured tracer at me and I took poor view of it. Ran out of ammunition.

A shot of *Melbourne Star* hidden by bomb splashes, Operation Pedestal, August 1942. (David Macfarlane)

Lovell shot down one Stuka, the dive bomber ditching in the sea with some difficulty, with both occupants being thrown out. Claims were also made for a Ju 87 damaged by Mejor and Flight Sergeant Pinney, but Flight Sergeant Buntine failed to return. It was discovered later that gunners on one of the surviving merchantmen, the *Dorset*, had shot down the 24-year-old Australian's Spitfire by mistake.

Captain Tuckett aboard the *Dorset* recalled:

These guns were placed around the ship and were not fitted with any means of communication, hence it was impossible to establish any sort of control. The officer on the bridge saw Spitfires overhead but was unable to communicate with the gun's crew, and within a few seconds one of our own Spitfires was shot down. When friendly aircraft is mistaken for hostile and fire is opened, I think it would reassure the gunners if the aircraft turned away, reported the *Dorset*'s liaison officer. The Spitfires continued over the ship in a steep bank and although several officers including myself ordered ceasefire we had the misfortune to shoot one down.

If Buntine had lived to tell his story he might have said he simply could not bloody believe the gunners could not distinguish a Spitfire on the tail of a Stuka. Equally, the *Dorset* gunners were told that if they saw a plane, it was the enemy so shoot it. Friendly planes, they were told, would not fly over the convoy and they did not believe they had air cover, so they blazed away at anything they saw. Such are the tragedies and fortunes of war.

Slightly later, what was identified as an Italian SM 84 bomber was encountered with an escort of six fighters. The bomber was claimed as shot down by Pinney – but this turned out to be a German Dornier (Do) 24 seaplane which reported being attacked by Spitfires and managed to alight safely at Marsala despite the damage caused.

1. No. 22 EFTS Trinity Hall
Cambridge. (J.G. Mejor)

2. No. 132 Squadron, Peterhead,
Scotland, 1941. (J.G. Mejor)

3. J.G. Mejor and visiting Hurricane to 132 Squadron, Peterhead, 1942. (J.G. Mejor)

4. John Mejor prior to posting to Malta, 1942. (J.G. Mejor)

5. In pensive mood: J.G. Mejor, 1942. (J.G. Mejor)

6. USS *Wasp*, the American aircraft carrier for Operation Calendar from which John Mejor took off for Malta, 20 April 1942. (Imperial War Museum A9232)

7. Engine of Spitfire 3-M being warmed up and tested on the flight deck of USS *Wasp*. Note the men on the tail to prevent tail rise during the operation. HMS *Eagle* in the background, April 1942. (US National Archive)

8. Grumman Martlett and Spitfires lined up on deck of USS *Wasp*, Operation Calendar, April 1942. (US National Archive)

9. Burnt out Hurricane, Malta, 1942. (J.G. Mejor)

10. Burnt out Beaufighter, Malta 1942. (J.G. Mejor)

11. At readiness, Malta, 1942. (J.G. Mejor)

12. Pilot Officer Michael Graves on the roof of the mess half-cut, 126 Squadron, Malta, 1942. (J.G. Mejor)

13. Pilot Officer J.G. Mejor, 126 Squadron, Malta, 1942. (J.G. Mejor)

14. Bristol Beaufighter, Malta, 1942. (J.G. Mejor)

15. Valletta Harbour and Bofors gun, Malta, 1942. (Imperial War Museum GM946)

16. No. 126 Squadron, Malta, 1942. (J.G. Mejor)

17. Lord Gort leading the investiture in front of the Castille Valletta, 1942. (Imperial War Museum GM1361)

18. *Melbourne Star* hidden by bomb splashes, Operation Pedestal, August 1942. (David Macfarlane)

19. And they lined the barricades: welcome reception, Operation Pedestal, August 1942. (Author's collection)

20. Captain David Macfarlane OBE and DSC. (David Macfarlane)

Reference:-
HQMED/489/1044/D.O.

Headquarters,

R.A.F. MEDITERRANEAN.

Dear Captain,

Will you please accept the congratulations of the Royal Air Force, Malta, on the grand performance put up by your ship in reaching Malta in spite of every form of attack by the enemy.

My Fighter Squadrons were giving you fighter cover from dawn yesterday, 13th August. They had been told to ~~meet~~ the convoy at about 120 miles from Malta but had no serious difficulty in reaching you at about 180 miles from shore.

My Squadrons are anxious to know whether the fighter protection from dawn, 13th August, was effective. In the absence of either of the directing ships, Cairo or Nigeria, our fighters could not be given indication of approaching enemy raids, at least, not until the convoy reached about 50 miles from Malta.

My pilots would welcome an opportunity of seeing you and thanking you personally for bringing your ship through.

Would you like to pay a visit to some of my Aerodromes next Thursday, 20th August, departing at 1600 hours, having tea at one of the Aerodromes and having a look around, then returning with me to my house for drinks? We could then fix you up for dinner in our Mess and return you to your ship or shore billet later.

If you are too busy for letter writing please let me know by telephone - Arial Exchange, Extension 1.

Thank you again for the very fine performance put up by your ship's company in bringing your ship safely to Malta.

Yours sincerely

K. R. Park

Captain Macfarlane,
M/V Melbourne Star.

From: Air Vice Marshal K.R.PARK, C.B., M.C., D.F.C.,

21. Letter from Air Vice Marshal Keith Park CB, MC and DFC to Captain Macfarlane MV *Melbourne Star*. (David Macfarlane)

22. David and Jenny Macfarlane. (David Macfarlane)

23. Spitfire IX, 122 Squadron, 1943. (J.G. Mejor)

24. 'And I came in behind him like this.' J.G. Mejor, 122 Squadron, 1944. (J.G. Mejor)

25. J.G. Mejor and Wing Commander Flying G.R.A.M. 'Robin' Johnston, 122 Wing, 2nd Tactical Air Force, 1944. (J.G. Mejor)

26. Test pilots of 39 Maintenance Unit, Colerne, 1944. (J.G. Mejor)

27. John and Cecile in the RAF in post-war Germany. (J.G. Mejor)

28. John and Cecile in the RAF in Canada after the war. (J.G. Mejor)

At about 11.20 a.m. another force of twenty Italian SM 79s escorted by Macchi C 202 fighters attacked, the fighters engaged by Spitfires while the SM 79 dive bombers deployed to commence their attacks. One dropped his torpedo at extreme range but the others seemed determined to press home their attacks at closer range. They flew at masthead height but fire from HMS *Pathfinder* and the rest of the convoy threw the Italians off their approaches and most of the torpedoes missed their targets, save one which became entangled in the paravane of the *Port Chalmers'* mine-sweeping gear. This left the *Port Chalmers'* Captain Pinkney in the tricky position of having a live torpedo swinging in the wires of its paravane and with the distinct possibility it could detonate against the side of the ship at any moment. In the end the para-vane was unshackled and heaved over the side with its dangerous cargo, whereupon it sank to the bottom and exploded at about 400 fathoms. Although the ship was well clear, the explosion was still enough to lift it out of the water.

During the same dive-bombing attack, the *Dorset* came to grief, struck aft by a heavy bomb which penetrated No. 4 hold and flooded the engine room. A fire started in the hold, next to the hold with the high-octane fuel, and as the electric pumps failed there was no option but to abandon ship. The ship was supposed to have been scuttled but the charges were left in a flooded part of the ship so she was abandoned and left to burn. Lifeboats were lowered and all the crew were picked up by HMS *Bramham*. *Rochester Castle* was again damaged by near misses and the force of the explosions shut down her engines, with another fire raging out of control which threatened the magazine, that had to be flooded to bring the fire under control.

Further Spitfire patrols were maintained and the pilots con-tinued to report engagements. A section of four Spitfires from 249 Squadron patrolled the convoy at around 2 p.m. but were fired upon by the convoy escorts, and Flight Sergeant Tommy

Parks – a tough-talking Canadian – had to bail out and was pulled from the sea by the escort that had shot him down.

After picking up the crew of the *Dorset*, HMS *Bramham* returned to protect what was left of the convoy, now a mere three ships. The destroyers *Penn* and *Ledbury* were sent back to find the becalmed *Ohio*. By now the convoy was in range of the short-range Spitfires from Malta, and despite repeated attempts they managed to keep the bombers away and by 2.30 p.m. the Malta escort force made contact to reinforce the convoy escort.

Macfarlane, on board *Melbourne Star*, recalled:

> The raids were continuous until the early afternoon when they suddenly ceased. Later we were met by the Malta escort, consisting of minesweepers and motor torpedo boats. We were taken over for our entry into Malta. The cruisers and destroyers then turned and proceeded back to Gibraltar. After the Malta escort took over we proceeded the rest of the way without further excitement, arriving there about 6 p.m. on 13 August. Only two other ships came in with us, the SS *Rochester Castle* and the SS *Port Chalmers*.

For the *Port Chalmers*, *Rochester Castle* and *Melbourne Star* the worst of their ordeal was now over and by 4 p.m. they had Malta in sight.

Towards the end of the afternoon there were several more contacts. At around 5 p.m. Squadron Leader Lovell claimed an SM 84 shot down, and 2 hours later Flight Sergeant Macnamara and Sergeant Jim Hawkins claimed another. Flight Sergeant Alan Scott recalled the events of the day and claimed what he thought was an Italian Breda (Ba) 88:

> We escorted the Malta convoy on 13 and 14 August. Raid came in with a Breda and six 109s and some Italian fighters. I got my sights on the Breda and destroyed it when I got a 3 second burst in his petrol tank. A mass of flames and he went straight into the

drink. I flew through the wreckage. No survivors. While this was happening the ships were pooping off at everything they could find and flak clouds from them were highly dangerous from our point of view!

The Italians lost two more of their reconnaissance aircraft to 1435 Squadron late in the afternoon. Mejor was led to believe he had clobbered one when flying with Flight Lieutenant Wally Mcleod, who in turn himself claimed an Me 109 which crashed onto the island of Pantelleria, killing the pilot.

> Log Book: Spitfire VB Scramble. Patrol tanker *Ohio* and *SS Brisbane Star*, both disabled. Italian rescue flying boat (like the one we captured) looking for stray WOPS. Myself and No. 2 did dummy attack to make sure his crosses were red. He panicked. We flew across him waggling wings. Shook him! Mac went after a 109 down on drink but could not catch him. Mac used bad language on RT. Three Ju 88s came in and dropped bombs. We chased them for short while. I fired 3 second burst but saw no results. Pity! No. 3 and No. 4 had squirt at one each but they did not claim as they saw no results. (Y Service thinks we got all three – good show, hope they all bought it.)

Wellum again records, 'Late in the afternoon Basil and I fly a standing patrol over Grand Harbour until relieved by another pair. We see no sign of the enemy and no sign of any ships coming into the harbour.'

> Log Book: Spitfire VB Scramble. More convoy patrol nothing doing.

By 6.25 p.m. the group of three surviving merchantmen slowly steamed into Grand Harbour, welcomed by thousands of cheering Maltese and servicemen, with bands playing at the harbour entrance. Unused to any fanfare at times of arrival or departure,

*Rochester Castle* was first, with a great gaping hole in her side, followed by *Port Chalmers* and then *Melbourne Star*.

In Valletta itself a young Maltese boy, Charles Grech, remembered the arrival of the first ships of the convoy:

> On 13 August, in the afternoon, my friends and I were at Fort Ghadir on the Sliema promenade when we made out three cargo ships and some warships on the horizon, slowly approaching Grand Harbour. These were *Port Chalmers*, *Rochester Castle* and *Melbourne Star*. The incredulous watchers, who happened to be on the waterfront, could not believe their eyes. Then as the full meaning of the sight sank in, they gradually started clapping, cheering and waving their handkerchiefs, thanking god for the safe arrival of these ships. The soldiers manning the harbour defences were reassured that at least they would now have enough ammunition for their guns. Some RFA [Royal Fleet Auxiliary] pilots gathered in front of the Meadow Bank Hotel and the Crown Hotel were cheering their heads off at the sight of the arrival of the ships. They were throwing their caps in the air and prancing around. Word spread like wildfire and many flocked to the Valletta bastions to welcome these war heroes. A military band on the Lower Barracca played the ships in. All of them bore the scars of war. As they entered Grand Harbour they looked battered, charred, rusty and holed and appeared to be in immediate danger of sinking.

The *Rochester Castle* had been hit again and again, and with two fires still burning in her holds, seamen climbed in amid ammunition that could blow at any second and extinguished the flames as the captain maintained speed. 'The whole of my crew behaved magnificently throughout the many sustained and violent attacks,' reported Captain Richard Wren.

The *Melbourne Star* was missing the thirty-three men who had jumped overboard into a burning sea when the *Waimarama* blew up in front of her earlier that morning. Ten of them perished in the sea from the flames they thought they were avoiding. Macfarlane reported:

> The fighting spirit of the ship was magnificent, every single man on board made all effort throughout to fight off the enemy, the hotter the battle became, the stouter, if possible, were their efforts. I cannot say too much for the officers and crew.

Macfarlane was blown away by the reception they received. Happy and relieved to have survived, he watched the Maltese people lining the docks, ramparts and the Barrakkas, cheering and waving flags, and only then did he realise what it meant to the islanders. It was a sight he would never forget and he and many exhausted, grimy and hungry merchant seamen found the occasion deeply affecting. 'We thought we must have done something significant' was the overriding emotion, as the cheers finally released each of the sailors from the frightening tension they had endured over the past few days. Most had been on continuous action stations for over 36 hours.

Geoffrey Wellum had also made his way down to the harbour:

> Four battered but defiant ships enter Grand Harbour escorted by some destroyers. What a battle these boys have been through. I recognise three of the ships. They had been stealing close to the *Furious* and their names are the *Melbourne Star*, *Brisbane Star* and *Port Chalmers*. The fourth I don't recognise but she is pretty big. Surely these four can't be all that's left of that proud convoy? The central figure of the whole saga is, of course, the tanker *Ohio* and she is still adrift somewhere.

The joy of the Maltese is total.

In Valletta, detailed preparations had been made beforehand for the unloading of what cargo made it to Malta. Stevedores, lorries, barges and empty warehouses were all ready to receive the stock

*Melbourne Star* arriving at Valletta Harbour. (David Macfarlane)

*Melbourne Star* arriving at Valletta Harbour. (Author's collection)

of supplies that had been so long in coming. After sunset there was an unusual glow above Valletta, Floriana and Grand Harbour, the likes of which had not been seen since the onset of the war. It was the glow of arc lights to illuminate the docks during the unloading operation, ensuring that work could continue throughout the night.

Three ships out of fourteen had made it, but to the west there remained a further three ships of the convoy still afloat and all attention was now to be focused on efforts to get those three – *Ohio*, *Dorset* and *Brisbane Star* – into Malta. Meanwhile, the remaining ships of Force X steamed at full speed back towards Gibraltar. Led by HMS *Ashanti* with Admiral Burrough on board, they steered clear of the smoking, stationary remains of the *Ohio* in order that any aircraft shadowing the *Ohio* could be avoided. The *Ohio* remained a lame duck 12 miles off of the island of Linosa.

The *Brisbane Star* had been on her own for most of the daylight hours of 13 August. She was down in the water by her head with almost 10ft of water in her hold after being torpedoed on the 12th and was slowly moving at about 8 knots, which was too slow for her to rejoin the convoy. Her Captain, N.F. Riley, had decided to try and proceed to Malta independently by the inshore route off the coast of Vichy-controlled Tunisia. At daybreak she was spotted by an Italian SM 79 torpedo bomber from Sicily but as she was within the territorial waters of Tunisia, under the rules of war, neither the ship nor the aeroplane could fire unless fired upon. There followed a period of bluff and counter-bluff with the SM 79 making dummy runs to attempt to get *Brisbane Star* to fire, but after three dummy runs the pilot gave up and went to search for alternative targets. Captain Riley noted in his report that the Italian pilot was a gentleman and observed the rules of war, but nevertheless expected the Italian to report his position and was sure the *Luftwaffe* would not be quite so forgiving. In the event, no further aircraft arrived and later that morning the signal station at Hammamet tried to contact *Brisbane Star* with flag signals. It was also a rule of war (and still is) that ships sailing in territorial waters should display their call sign letters which determines their nationality. All attempts by the signal station to recognise *Brisbane Star* were not helped by Riley's answers, which confused the French, but he realised he could not bluff forever so moved out of territorial waters. He then noticed he was being shadowed by a submarine but had no method of determining its nationality, so entered territorial waters once more, only to be ordered to stop by a French patrol boat. When he did not, the patrol boat fired a shot across his bows and Captain Riley had no choice but to stop. The *Brisbane Star* was boarded by two Vichy French officers who insisted that he should follow them to Tunisia, where his ship would be seized and the crew interned for the rest of war. Captain Riley was not easily ruffled and invited the officers down to his cabin, where he plied them with whisky and his Irish charm and managed to persuade them not to proceed with their plans. Instead they allowed him to carry on and took one of the badly injured crewmen to hospital for treatment, where sadly, he died from his wounds. By now night was falling and *Brisbane Star* was able to shake off the submarine in the shallow waters near the coast and made her way steadily towards Malta.

The burning *Dorset* was less fortunate. She had been abandoned after being bombed earlier in the day, fire broke out and water had flooded the engine room. Her crew had been picked up by HMS *Bramham* but she continued to burn close by the *Ohio* and lay dead in the water, helpless against repeated attempts by the *Luftwaffe* to finish her off. Despite her immobilisation she refused to go down, so Captain J.C. Tuckett re-boarded his ship to see if it was possible to get her to Malta. He reluctantly decided that it was impossible due to the damage and the intense heat from the fires – in any event, the decision on whether to even try was taken out of his hands when she was hit by a bomb from a group of Ju 88s who scored a direct hit at around 6 p.m. She settled down by her stern and by 8 p.m. had gone, sinking with her colours flying, including the traditional red duster. A sad and melancholy sight.

The *Ohio* was also in a bad way. Her precious cargo of fuel was still largely intact but a large piece of her side was sticking out and she had the remains of two German bombers on her decks (a Ju 87 and Ju 88). When the destroyer *Penn* tried to tow her, the large piece of steel plating sticking out acted like a rudder and she went round in circles. Attacked again by Ju 88s, another near miss caused further damage and she was in danger of splitting herself in two. With her engines stopped, the decision was taken to abandon ship. HMS *Penn* circled the stricken tanker but with standing patrols of Spitfires from Malta, including 1435 Squadron, the *Ohio* did not sink and was only hit once more; this time the bomb wrecked the engine room and the rudder. The crew, having re-boarded the ship in an attempt to move her, had to abandon her for a second time.

By evening the Germans had called a halt to their attacks on the remnants of the convoy and concentrated on the returning Force X to Gibraltar. *Bramham* had picked up the *Dorset* survivors and was sent to look for HMS *Manchester* but, unable to find her, returned to help with *Ohio*. *Ledbury* was also on hand to help.

## 14 AUGUST 1942

After dark the previous evening another attempt was made to get the stricken tanker *Ohio* moving. Lieutenant Commander Swain from HMS *Penn* took charge of the situation – Captain Mason and the rest of his crew from *Ohio* had been evacuated to the *Penn* because they were shattered and had not slept in nearly three days. Swain and Lieutenant Commander Baines from HMS *Bramham*, together with the minesweeper HMS *Rye* from Malta, attempted to tow her in. Conventional towing from ahead was tried again without success. Baines suggested that the destroyers should be lashed either side of the *Ohio* as this would provide forward movement but also help in steering the ship, but *Penn* was unable to secure properly because of the steel plating protruding from the side of the tanker so it was decided to wait for daybreak.

A motor launch, *ML 168*, had also taken on board thirty-three of the *Ohio* crew the previous evening to give them a break, but during the night had developed engine trouble and returned to Malta. When the crew members woke the following morning to find themselves in Valletta Harbour they were both surprised and angry as they believed they had unwittingly abandoned ship. Amongst these men were most of the officers and engineers.

At daybreak most of the rescued men onboard *Bramham* and *Penn* again boarded *Ohio* to man the guns, clear the wreckage and generally help wherever they could with towlines. Attempts were made to get the *Ohio* moving but constant air attacks were forcing the destroyers to break away and engage the bombers. Spitfires from Malta were also engaged.

At about 9 a.m. another near miss aft of the tanker carried away her rudder and holed the shell plating further, and although no direct hits were made and little damage was caused, the attacks did cause much frustration and confusion amongst the escort craft, with broken tow ropes and slip wires. HMS *Ledbury* had by now returned from its search for HMS *Manchester* and was able to provide assistance.

By mid-morning a further attack was made by five Ju 87s escorted by twenty-three MC 202s that arrived over the tanker, but it was by now protected by standing patrols of Malta Spitfires, including those from 229 and 1435 Squadrons.

Mejor Log Book: Spitfire VB Fighter Sweep Angels 30.

Squadron ORB. It is to be feared that the tanker which claimed so much attention yesterday continued to be a 'thorn in the flesh' to the enemy. No less than six formations were airborne during the day to protect it. At 10.20 enemy aircraft appeared on this sortie and the Squadron score was further augmented:

One Ju 87 destroyed by Sqn Leader Lovell and Sgt Philp.

One RE 2001 destroyed by F/Sgt Maclennan [incorrectly identified as an RE 2001, it was an MC 202].

One Ju 87 destroyed by Sgt Philip

Squadron Leader Lovell reported:

As we arrived I saw one Ju 87 diving and went for it, overtook it rapidly, opened fire at 300 yards and broke away at 30 yards. I saw strikes all over the engine and fuselage. White smoke poured from both sides. He lost height, the smoke stopped and he did a steep turn to port and flew west, losing height. I turned back towards the tanker and saw the Ju 87 crash into the sea. I claim a half share with Sergeant Philp.

Ian 'Mac' Maclennan reported:

Started firing from 150 yards to 25 yards. Saw many strikes all along the top of the aircraft. White smoke started pouring out, he turned very slowly to the left, nose slightly up. I closed into 15ft or less, firing all over the cockpit and pieces flew off again. His nose dropped and he kept turning slowly to the left, going down, trailing thick white smoke. I claim this aircraft as destroyed as I think the pilot was dead.

In fact the pilot, an Italian, was picked up later after he bailed out by a German Do 24 rescue plane.

By about 11 a.m. *Penn* had been secured to the starboard side, *Bramham* to the port side and *Rye* was towing ahead, and slowly but surely *Ohio* began to inch towards harbour at about 6 knots.

Captain Mason went back on board to assess the damage; air compressors from *Penn* had been placed on board to pump air into the cargo tanks and pumps from the *Penn* were also pumping water from the engine room, which greatly improved *Ohio*'s freeboard as this was only about 2ft above the waterline. After his inspection, Mason believed that they could save the tanker. He thought she might be able to stay afloat for another 12 hours thanks to the work done by the *Penn*'s engineers and even if the tanker did break her back by the pump room, then the aft part would sink but the forward section would remain afloat and at least 70 per cent of her fuel and oil could be saved.

The vessels lashed together continued their tortuous journey for the rest of the day until about 8 p.m. when they were met by the tug *Robust* from Valleta, to which they were supposed to hand over the towing duties. The tug connected a line to the *Ohio* and started to tow, but the tug master did not appreciate the effect this would have on the deadweight that the *Ohio* was. The power exerted caused the tug to veer at the end of its tow rope in the arc of a circle, to such an extent that it swung through 180 degrees and rammed HMS *Penn*, holing her above the waterline. Captain Swain on the *Penn* was suitably unimpressed and ordered the tug to return to Valletta while the destroyers continued the tow themselves. After what seemed an eternity they arrived at the entrance to the swept channel into Valletta at around 2 a.m.

## 15 AUGUST 1942

Through the night the ships, lashed together, moved slowly towards Valletta at around 4 knots. As the night progressed more ships came out from Valletta to help, including three more tugs. These were needed because of the difficulty in turning the tanker in the dangerous waters close to Malta that contained the protective minefields. Cautiously, the *Penn* and *Bramham* nursed the tanker round, then *Ledbury* came alongside and passed a 6in wire to try and pull the three ships round again and two of the motor launches did their best to push the tanker in an agonising battle to move her safely through the minefield. By 6 a.m. they had made the safety of the channel into the harbour and by 8 a.m. they had passed through the entrance to a rapturous welcome. Again the battlements were lined with cheering throngs of Maltese and servicemen, with a band playing to accompany them. Even so, the last mile seemed never-ending as the decks of the tanker were awash and her torn hull was protesting, creaking and groaning from the strain being put upon it. There was still a fear, even in the safety of the harbour, that she might sink and block the harbour.

*Penn* was cast off and the *Branham* remained alongside to guide her the final few hundred yards to her berth and finally she made it, next to the wreck of another tanker, the *Plumleaf*, which lay with its superstructure just visible above the waterline. *Bramham* then cast off and a Royal Navy Auxillary, the *Boxol*, slid the tanker into place and dockyard men and stevedores immediately swarmed aboard her with pumps and pipes to unload the vital cargo before she had a chance to settle and break her back.

This most poignant scene was remembered by Charles Grech:

Early in the morning of 15 August, the mid-summer feast of Santa Maria, the large tanker loomed on the horizon, very pain-fully edging its way towards Grand Harbour. It was down in the water and supported on either side by the destroyers HMS *Penn* and HMS *Ledbury*. The minesweeper HMS *Rye* was towing her, the heroine of the convoy laden with kerosene, oil and aviation fuel which were so badly needed. This morning I had planned to go to swim with my friends on the shore by the Sliema Point bat-tery but on seeing the *Ohio*, we quickly decided to go and watch it enter Grand Harbour. We rushed down to the Strand to board the ferry and crossed over to Valletta. There we hurried up the steps to the city and down to the Lower Barracca gardens; these were already overcrowded with people, anxious to see the tanker safely enter between the breakwater arms. Groups of men were debating whether she would make it up the breakwater, some even predicted that she would sink to the bottom and there was nothing left inside her tanks other than seawater!

Just after 9 a.m. the *Ohio* was literally carried between the breakwater arms, still supported by the two destroyers and nursed along by tug boats. She was charred from the fires and her iron works were twisted and she was holed in many places, presenting a terrible sight. The crowds on the bastions and the barraccas were at first silent, but then they exploded into an orgy of cheering, clapping, shouting and waving Maltese flags and Union Jacks to the accompaniment of the military band playing from the Lower Barracca bastion.

Mejor Log Book: Spitfire VB Scramble, plot on board but did not come in. Squadron stayed and patrolled halfway to Sicily and Harbour – we got damn cold. Angels 24

It was whilst at dispersal that the squadron had news that another ship was in. Geoffrey Wellum records:

Rumour has it that she is the *Ohio*. If true Malta is saved. It was later confirmed that it was indeed the *Ohio* but so extensively damaged that two destroyers, one lashed to either side, brought her in at 3 knots. Their pumps barely keeping her afloat. She had been hit by bombs, torpedoes and it is said that a Ju 87 crashed into her deck. Many of her crew have died and there are fires still burning. Her cargo of fuel is intact.

Squadron ORB – Whilst on search for Sgt Buntine who was missing one Cant 5066 and one SM84 were attacked. At 09.25 six Me109s were encountered 25 miles east of Zonkor point but no claims were recorded. Rest of day was spent doing patrols over Grand Harbour.

Unloading continued uninterrupted. The *Boxol* continued to pump some of the fuel into her own tanks, which made the fore tanks lighter and the aft part of the tanker heavier and threatened to break her in half. In addition, it was now fully light and there was the distinct possibility of further bombing attacks from the *Luftwaffe* – in the event none came. No attempts were made to disrupt the unloading. Already the *Rochester Castle*, *Port Chalmers* and *Melbourne Star* had completed being discharged, and the *Brisbane Star*, which had reached safety the previous day, was close to being emptied.

The Spitfires continued to provide a protective umbrella and the *Ohio* fuel tanks were cleared and emptied before she finally gave in and settled quietly on the bottom of Valletta Harbour. She never sailed again.

Operation Pedestal had been a monumental and bitter battle, fought by the Allies with a touch of desperation. Of the fourteen merchant ships that set out, nine had been sunk and the Royal Navy had lost an aircraft carrier, the *Eagle*, and two cruisers, the *Manchester* and *Cairo*. Two of the other carriers, *Indomitable* and *Victorious*, were damaged and the destroyer *Foresight* was sunk by torpedo. At the price of great sacrifice and suffering, the Royal Navy and merchant seamen had brought the convoy through and raised the siege of Malta. The enemy had failed to do what it set out to, which was prevent the Allies from relieving the beleaguered and gallant island of Malta.

Both Johnnie Mejor and David Macfarlane had played their part, though neither was aware of the other's involvement at this stage.

## MALTA – POST-OPERATION PEDESTAL

Operation Ceres, the plan to ensure the swift discharge of the valuable cargo from the five surviving merchant ships, was implemented as soon as they arrived in Valletta to reduce the chances of damage by Axis aircraft , should they have attacked. The fact that they did not attack made a great difference – 32,000 tons of general cargo were unloaded and stored safely by 22 August using stevedores, troops and policeman, which ensured Malta could survive for at least another two months.

Churchill summed up the effort and sacrifice made:

> Thus in the end five gallant merchant ships out of fourteen got through with their precious cargoes. The loss of nearly 450 men, of so many of the finest ships in the Merchant Navy and in the escorting fleet of the Royal Navy was grievous. The reward justified the price exacted. Replenished with vital ammunition and vital stores the strength of Malta was revived.

The masters and crews were treated like royalty by the people of Malta. Complimentary tickets were offered by the management of the Manoel Theatre and local cinemas to any of the crew members. In return 'Mac', as one of the masters, hosted food and drinks on board the *Melbourne Star* shortly after they arrived for the RAF pilots who had helped protect the convoy. *Melbourne Star* was still more than adequately stocked with food, despite their ordeal, and by then Johnnie Mejor was aware that his uncle David Macfarlane was captain of one of the ships that had got through. Mejor and his good friend Alan Scott went down to Valletta, having been invited on board ship. They were starving and the prospect of food and a cold beer was too good to be true.

On board, Macfarlane was welcoming people aboard. Mejor, with a big smile and brimming moustache, went up to shake his uncle's hand – 'Hello Uncle Mac,' he beamed. Macfarlane was taken aback; he clearly did not know his nephew was there. 'Little Johnnie,' he replied, 'I didn't know you were going to be here, well I'm blown, was that you up there, helping us to get through?' 'Certainly was,' Mejor replied. A cold beer was the order of the day, but neither Mejor nor Macfarlane were big drinkers, yet they were able to enjoy each other's company and recall each other's involvement in a quite extraordinary tale of courage and superhuman effort to get the merchant ships and the tanker *Ohio* through to Malta.

Frank Hewlett, a crew member of *Ledbury*, recounted a simple story that brought out the human element and highlighted the bond between the military personnel and the Maltese:

We remained in Malta anchored off Senglea for about 10 days. I happened to come into the Mess one afternoon for the usual mug of tea and was surprised to see two members of the Royal Malta Artillery sitting at the Mess table. I was hailed by one of the shipmates as 'Lofty the pipe smoker'. Although the two gunners had already been supplied with cigarettes, one of them was a pipe smoker and yearned for some decent pipe tobacco. I handed him my pouch. Remembering I also had made up a perique approx. two months previously, I went to my locker and cut the perique in half and handed it to him, saying 'there you go Tommy, there is about 6 ounces of quality leaf tobacco there, and if you go carefully, it should last until the siege is lifted'. He wanted to pay for it but as leaf tobacco was only 1s 6d a pound I wouldn't accept a penny. I felt rather embarrassed on seeing him almost in tears: after all we had been under attack for 5 days or so, but the Maltese have been sticking it out for almost 2 years. Before we sailed from Malta, *Ledbury*, *Bramham* and *Penn* landed their stores of food except for 2 days' rations and all their NAAFI supplies and delivered them to Fort St Angelo. Just a drop of water in the ocean but a token of the respect the Navy felt for those they leave behind on the island of Malta.

The arrival of the five ships was hailed as a triumph. The British press praised the Merchant and Royal Navies on their achievement, even though losses were high. The Maltese rose to the occasion. The masters and crews found warm hospitality from the Maltese. Lord Gort received them at San Anton Palace while they were also entertained by several clubs, institutions and families. As the convoy was concluded on 15 August, when *Ohio* eventually reached Valletta Harbour, it became known as IL-Konvoj ta' Santa Marija, the date of the Feast of the Assumption.

On 17 August a further batch of Spitfire reinforcements were flown in from the carrier *Furious*, which made a second run from Gibraltar under the codename Operation Baritone. They were led in by experienced pilots from Malta, Flight Lieutenant Halford, Flight Officer McElroy and Pilot Officers Evans and Parkinson. Although Mejor flew on the 17th to patrol Grand Harbour again, what proved to be his last flight on Malta was uneventful. The influx of reinforcement pilots allowed further releases of tour-expired men, Mejor being one of them. His CO, Tony Lovell, was the one to tell him. Mejor could not believe it; four months near enough, he had done his 200 operational hours, he was tour-expired and shattered, but he was being sent home to England tomorrow, via Gibraltar. What a joy. Was it a cruel joke? No, he was definitely going. If there was a time for a drink it was that night in the Mess, so he did and early the following morning, still in darkness, he boarded the Hudson, blacked out for the trip to Gibraltar. His fellow passengers included Les Watts and Ossie Linton from 249 Squadron, Geoff Northcott, Eric Dicks Sherwood and Forster and Smith, who was suffering from hepatitis, from 229 Squadron, and the American Reade Tilley from Mejor's old squadron, No. 126.

With blackout curtains drawn across the windows and no lights of any kind allowed in the cabin, they took off from Malta.

Imprisoned in darkness, they passed Pantelleria and south of Sardinia, beyond the threat of the Me 109s. They made slow, monotonous progress, accompanied by the drone of engines, vibrating wings and a sunrise to beat all others. With the quiet in the fuselage, his fellow pilots also shattered, sleep was needed. As the sun rose he could just make out the rusty haze of Algiers and the mountains. And then, slowly but surely, the unmistakeable sight of the Rock. There it was. Seven and a half hours after taking off from Malta, the Hudson safely landed in Gibraltar. Stumbling, almost falling down the Hudson's steps, Mejor yawned, stretched and heaved a huge sigh of relief. He had survived.

## NEW CHAPTER

A preliminary report on the convoy was written by M. Ford, Vice Admiral Malta, on 22 August, marked most secret. In its summary he concluded:

a   Towage of *Ohio* was outstanding feet of courage, determination, and good seamanship on part of all concerned and particularly *Penn*, *Bramham*, *Ledbury* and *Rye* and Commander of M/S who conducted operations during final day and last critical night.

b   Considering position and extreme value of cargo [the] weakness of enemy air attacks and complete absence of surface or submarine attack is remarkable. Seems probable that Axis Air Forces had suffered such heavy casualties that they were unable to stage or unprepared to risk a full scale attack.

c   Aircraft from Malta worked ceaselessly and answered every call made to utmost limit of their ability.

In recent convoy to Malta there were a number of Merchant Navy Captains, some who distinguished themselves. The opposition was probably greater than on any previous occasion. The Admiralty proposes to seek approval for awards forthwith to the Vice Admiral Commanding and the two Rear Admirals. It is agreed to be of the utmost importance that some Honours for the Masters of the Merchant Navy vessels in the convoy should be awarded at the same time. The following have been specially selected:

DSO Captain D.R. Macfarlane OBE – SS *Melbourne Star*,
    Captain D.W. Mason – SS *Ohio*,
    Captain F.N. Riley –SS *Brisbane Star*,
    Captain R. Wren – SS *Rochester Castle*.

A statement of services is attached. It is desired to obtain approval for these awards at the earliest possible moment. I suggest that if you concur and the Prime Minister sees fit, these four names should be submitted to His Majesty the King.

**Services Statement**
Captain D.R. Macfarlane – SS *Melbourne Star*, this officer showed great initiative and determination.

On 22 August the King replied:

The King has been graciously pleased to give orders for the under-mentioned promotion in, and appointments to, the Distinguished Service Order for services in the Merchant Navy during the passage to Malta of an important convoy.

Captain David Rattray Macfarlane OBE – Master, Captain Dudley William Mason – Master, Captain Frederick Neville Riley – Master.

The DSO awards were immediate and the first occasion on which they were awarded to Merchant Navy captains. Dudley Mason's award was later upgraded to the George Cross in September 1942.

On 26 August the rear admiral commanding Operation Pedestal in turn wrote to the office of the Vice Admiral Malta – marked top secret it read as follows: 'I have much pleasure in forwarding the following extract from a report by the Flag Officer Commanding Force H on the recent successful Operation which resulted in the safe arrival of a very valuable convoy.'

**Behaviour of MT Ships**

The Rear Admiral Commanding the 18th Cruiser Squadron reports that the Operation was successfully carried out due to, and in no small measure, the behaviour of the Merchant Ships in convoy. Their manoeuvring and general conduct caused me no anxiety whatsoever. I had complete confidence that orders given to them by me would be understood and promptly carried out. Their steadfast and resolute behaviour during air and U-boat attacks was most impressive and encouraging to us all. Particular credit is due to SS *Melbourne Star*, Commodore of the Convoy, who set a high standard and never failed to appreciate directly what he should do.

I should be grateful if you would inform the Captains of the Merchant Ships accordingly.

Back on Malta, the masters and officers of the five merchant ships were invited to a luncheon at the Casino Maltese on 4 September and five days later the business and mercantile community of Malta held a function at the Roxy Theatre at which the masters were presented with a silver model of a Gozo fishing boat and a silver watch inscribed 'For Valour and Devotion to Duty, Malta Convoy, August 1942'. The sense of generosity and appreciation from the Maltese was best shown by *The Times of Malta* on 21 August when it had launched the Malta Convoy Fund for the dependents of those men lost in the operation. Subscriptions big and small poured in from every town and village, every regiment on the island, so much so that when the fund closed on 12 October, it had raised the huge sum of £7,525 15 shillings.

When the enthusiasm had abated, Operation Pedestal caused ructions of a different nature back home. On the evidence of diary entries and from seamen who witnessed the loading of the cargo and packing cases stamped with Malta lying on the quays at Bristol, Liverpool and the Clyde, this basic lapse of security was referred to the Admiral of the Fleet and the subsequent inquiry held on behalf of the British Government resulted in the alteration to coding material destined for convoys.

Besides delivering badly needed supplies, the arrival of the convoy was a morale booster as the civilians and garrison realised they were not cut off from the rest of the Allied world. This did not mark the end of the siege of the island, however. The period of tightest rationing was from August to November 1942, when it was practically impossible to obtain anything but a few vegetables in addition to the rations. The aviation fuel delivered as part of Operation Pedestal enabled the RAF to intensify operations. In July and August 1942 over 120 Spitfires reached Malta, to be followed by Beaufighters and Wellingtons as Air Vice Marshal Park was determined to take the offensive back to the Germans and hit Rommel's supply chain where it hurt the most, his own convoys that were destined to supply the *Afrika Korps*. Many did not make it.

By 9 September the British press had got hold of the story of the convoy and the successful passage. The *Daily Mirror* on that day reported:

> Awards of the DSO for the first time in history to three Merchant Navy officers for heroism with the Malta Convoy were announced last night. They were preceded by a statement in Parliament that the splendid achievements of the Merchant Navy were now to be recognised by the awards of the DSO, Conspicuous Gallantry

Medal and Distinguished Service Medal, hitherto limited to the Services, to all heroes of the sea. The first three Merchant Navy officers to be awarded the DSO are Captain David Rattray Macfarlane of Ilford, Captain Frederick Neville Riley, an Australian, and Captain Richard Wren of Chipstead who showed 'fortitude, seamanship and endurance in taking Merchant Ships through to Malta in the face of relentless attacks by day and night from enemy submarines, aircraft and surface forces'.

Captain Macfarlane, who is 46, was about to take some belated leave when he heard an important job was in hand. Guessing it might be a Malta Convoy, he refused his leave because he was determined to see his ship through. At the height of the enemy attacks in the Mediterranean his only comment was, 'We set out for Malta and we are going through to Malta.'

Arriving in Malta, Captain Macfarlane took his Officers to a bar to buy them a drink and thanked them for bringing the ship through. Mrs Macfarlane told the *Daily Mirror* last night, 'I am proud of him, but I was just as proud before. I think every woman married to a man in the Merchant Service should be proud, for all these men are heroes. I last saw my husband in July. I knew he was off on an important job, something sticky he said, but I did not know what it was. I had a cable from him yesterday saying he was well.'

A letter from the Blue Star Line, the owners of the *Melbourne Star*, also arrived with Jenny Macfarlane, his wife, on 9 September:

Dear Mrs Macfarlane

We are all very pleased with the well-earned honour that has been conferred upon David, I shall look forward to the day when I can offer the big hand of congratulations to Captain David Macfarlane DSO, OBE.

You must feel very proud of him and of his gallantry.

With all good wishes

Captain David Rattray Macfarlane and Lord Gort of Malta, August 1942.
(David Macfarlane)

And then a further letter of congratulations arrived, also from the Blue Star Line:

Dear Mrs Macfarlane

I just wanted to send you, on behalf of the Blue Star Line, our congratulations at the distinction granted to your husband for his recent feat in navigating his ship safely to Malta.

You will of course have seen in the papers that he is to be awarded the Distinguished Service Order for this fine feat of seamanship, whilst his fellow master, Captain Riley, is to receive a similar decoration. That they are the first to receive this previously military decoration is unique in the history of the Merchant Marine Navy and we are very proud of that fact.

Yours sincerely

Then a few days later on 11 September a letter from the Combined Operations HQ in Whitehall arrived for Captain Macfarlane. It read:

Dear Captain Macfarlane

May I offer you my most sincere congratulations on one of the best earned DSOs of the war.

I am one of those who has been doing everything in their power to try and get the DSO thrown open to our gallant comrades in the Merchant Navy and I am therefore particularly glad to be able to write to one of the first recipients.

Yours sincerely

Louis Mountbatten

And finally, on 12 September, Lord John Gort himself from the palace in Malta wrote to Macfarlane:

Dear Captain Macfarlane

The news that his Majesty has been pleased to confer upon you the Distinguished Service Order has brought great pleasure to all of us here in Malta, and in particular to those of us who were privileged to watch your gallant vessel steaming into Grand Harbour undamaged by any of the furious attacks through which she had passed.

I hasten to send you my warmest congratulations.

Yours sincerely

Lord J.S. Gort

10282.

COMBINED OPERATIONS HEADQUARTERS,

1A. RICHMOND TERRACE,

WHITEHALL, S.W.1.

*Telephone :*
WHItehall 9777

11th September, 1942.

Dear Captain Macfarlane,

May I offer you my most sincere congratulations on one of the best earned D.S.O's of the war.

I am one of those who has been doing everything in their power to try and get the D.S.O. thrown open to our gallant comrades in the Merchant Navy and I am therefore particularly glad to be able to write to one of the first recipients.

Yours sincerely,

Louis Mountbatten

Captain David Rattray Macfarlane,
O.B.E., D.S.O.,

Master,
S.S.Melbourne Star,
c/o G.P.O.
London.

CCO/JP.

Meanwhile on the island Lord Gort was able to announce a very slight easing of the rationing. It was not much and food remained in short supply, but it was an indication that the grim deadline had not been reached and that the island could carry on in good heart and things would slowly get better. He added:

> Recently we have seen four merchant ships and an oil tanker reach Malta and this represents the largest number of ships that have arrived in Grand Harbour since September 1941. No sight could have been more welcome to all of us than the arrival of the convoy after so many anxious weeks of waiting and we all know that this great achievement was accomplished thanks to the dauntless courage of the Royal Navy, Merchant Navy and Royal Air Force.

With AVM Park determined to take the offensive back to the Germans and attack Rommel's supply convoys, nearly 100,000 tons of Rommel's urgently needed supplies were sent to the seabed in September 1942, depriving him of vital fuel and supplies at a critical point in the North African campaign.

The next month, October 1942, saw Montgomery make a stand at a little-known railway halt in Libya called El Alamein. Rommel was short of both fuel and supplies and was defeated, the first major victory by the Allies in the war. The tide had turned. Yet Malta, Rommel later admitted, was the rock on which all Axis hopes in the Mediterranean foundered, and this was in no small measure down to Pedestal. 'Mac' and Johnnie Mejor had played their part.

*Melbourne Star* remained in Malta for about six weeks. A slight illness prevented Macfarlane from joining the crew when she sailed back to Gibraltar but he was able to return to the UK and get some rest and see Jenny again.

Opposite: Letter from Louis Mountbatten in regard to the award of the DSO for David Macfarlane. (David Macfarlane)

6

# Rest and 2nd Tactical Air Force to D-Day

After a month off and complete rest, Johnnie Mejor was posted to No. 55 Operational Training Unit (OTU) at Annan in Scotland in September 1942, where he became an instructor and taught new pilots the art of flying. Annan was pretty inhospitable and a godforsaken place during the winter of 1942–43, but at least Mejor was still flying.

In charge of the OTU was Squadron Leader Dennis 'Hurricane' David. He had made his name in the Battle of France flying Hurricanes with 87 Squadron against overwhelming odds in the lost cause that culminated in the evacuation of the British Expeditionary Force from Dunkirk in May 1940. He continued to fly during the Battle of Britain and extended his score with further victories. By the time he was OC of the OTU he had been promoted to squadron leader; he was still only 23 and Mejor 22.

OTU training and flying was both intensive and demanding. It seems strange now to appreciate that instructors such as Mejor, although slightly older, had to impart their knowledge to new recruits only a few years younger than themselves. Sometimes they were just 18 or 19 and had very little flying time on the Hurricane, or no operational flying time at all and had been used to flying in the clear blue skies of the USA or Canada, not the treacherous flying conditions in Scotland and the rest of the UK. Accidents were both frequent and unfortunate, but Mejor's main role was to instil confidence into the young pilots of their ability to fly, and also to fight with their Hurricanes, even in vile weather conditions.

Knowing the system where experienced pilots back from operations were due a rest, Squadron Leader David did his best to put together as many pilots as he knew personally or who he knew something about, and in his own words managed to collect a wonderful cross-section of talent and personalities at the OTU. Mejor was recruited into this group of pilots, fitted in well and got on well with his CO.

The pupils to be trained as fighter pilots were arriving in their droves from their training units in Canada and the USA. 'They were extremely keen but very raw.' Mejor recalled. Low on flying time, the instructors gave them a couple of rides in a Miles Master dual trainer before letting them loose in a Hurricane, even a clapped out Hurricane. To them and Mejor, even as inexperienced instructors, some of these flights and checks took years off their lives. They could not believe there were so many hairy techniques in getting an aircraft into the air and down again. Pressure of time did not allow them to dally around giving basic instructions. Whenever a pupil displayed some ability, they were strapped into a Hurricane and the instructors stood back and prayed for the best. The results were often spectacular. Hurricanes staggered into the sky and, after a suitable pause 'gaining air experience', returned to attempt a landing. They attacked the runway from all angles. Some held off much too high and flat stalled with sickening thumps on squealing tyres; some swung off the landing areas and runways in a series of heart-stopping ground loops with the instructors watching, hoping that the pupils could at least stay within the confines of the airfield; and others came in so fast, too fast, and in a series of kangaroo jumps, it was only the mud at the end of the airfield that finally stopped them, and then the Hurricane would be standing vertically on the tip of its propeller. Although accidents were frequent, there were remarkably few casualties, which spoke volumes for the rugged construction of the Hurricane.

Having survived the first few days of instruction, new pupils – commonly known as kids – gradually got to grips with the Hurricanes. The instructors could then get down to imparting the knowledge required to get the kids to a standard where they could be released for operational flying as a squadron fighter pilot. All the basics such as battle formations, attacks, gunnery and Sailor Malan's famous ten rules were taught, and then in the final days of their course the kids were given mock fighter combats flying against an instructor.

This went on for nearly a year, only interrupted by a month away at No. 3 Flying Instructors School in December 1942 and January 1943, where he was assessed as average as a pilot and below average as a flying instructor. This bothered Mejor no end and his cause was taken up by his CO, David, who wrote in his log book, 'I do not agree, above average as a fighter pilot'.

In September 1943 Johnnie was posted back on operations and joined 122 Squadron at Kingsnorth near Ashford, back on Spitfires, this time the Mk IX, a much-improved aircraft. The squadron was led by Squadron Leader Pete Wickham DFC and bar. A graduate of the RAF College at Cranwell, Wickham had flown Gladiators in the Middle East with 33 Squadron before being posted to Greece with them, and came back to the UK with 72 Squadron as a flight commander and eventually commanded his own squadron, No. 111, in March 1942.

Kingsnorth had become operational in July that year when 65, 122 and 602 Squadrons arrived, but Mejor's introduction to the base was, to say the least, a little disconcerting. The driver who picked him up from the station took him over a little bridge and through a gateway. Ahead, he was greeted by a sea of mud which stretched for nearly a mile in each direction. The car and its occupants skidded, slithered and finally bounced onto some open metal track. Where were the hangars? There weren't any. Where were the living quarters? There were none. So what was there? The two metal track ways were the runways. There were tents to sleep in, one for the adjutant and a larger one to eat in and have mess. The Spitfires were kept under camouflage netting. Was this really it? Mejor did get a room in a cottage, but it was a derelict one that had been used as a piggery and may well still have been used, judging by the smells emanating from it.

122 Squadron was by this time part of the 2nd Tactical Air Force that was being formed to muster its resources prior to softening up 'Fortress Europe' for the planned invasion. They were there to find the best ways to ensure operations could go ahead from newly prepared strips after the planned invasion of France. Best described as primitive operating conditions, they did get a break for a couple of days when the runways deteriorated to such an extent that they were unusable and they were moved out to allow the Works Service Corps time to re-lay the runways.

It proved a short respite and Mejor's first operation with 122 Squadron was as top cover and escort in Spitfire IXs to B-26 Marauder bombers that attacked Evreux and Fauville on the evening of 24 September. It was a sign of things to come. Then, in an extraordinary coincidence, Allan Scott, Major's good friend from 1435 Squadron in Malta, was posted to No. 122 at Kingsnorth. No sooner had he joined the squadron than it was transferred to Weston Zoyland in Somerset. As it was close to the sea it was a suitable spot for air-firing practice on drogues, which were funnel-shaped devices similar to a windsock, towed by another aircraft, such as a Miles Martinet, to give pilots practice at shooting. This proved enjoyable and a bit different, as the drogues did not fire back at them like the Germans did and was good preparation for a return to operational flying. The posting also allowed the pilots to get to grips with Somerset cider or 'scrumpy' – its effects proving to be lethal compared to the normal pints of ale they were used to!

Back on operations, this time at Gravesend in Kent, they flew mostly fighter sweeps into France, hoping to get the *Luftwaffe* up into the air, or as an escort to bombers attacking various targets in northern France. The range of the Spitfire limited them to escorts into Northern France or the Frisian Islands – it did not allow them to escort the heavier bombers still bombing Germany.

Typical of the type of operations carried out are the following:

No. 122 Squadron, 2nd Tactical Air Force, in the build-up to D-Day, 1944.
(J.G. Mejor)

### 8 November 1943

Log Book – Spitfire IX – Top Cover but took off late. Target construction works between Calais and Boulogne with bombers Maurauders and Mitchells.

### 10 November 1943

Log Book – Spitfire IX – Cover to bombers, Maurauders, target Lille. No Hun fighters, quite a lot of flak.

**26 November 1943**

Log Book – Spitfire IX – Fighter Sweep & support to Bostons and Mitchells, target Audinghen, we were bounced near Methune by Me 109s and lost F/Sgt Bostock.

**30 November 1943**

Log Book – Spitfire IX – Withdrawal cover to 600 Forts. Rendezvous at Oostmalle – A little flak damned cold and bad visibility at base 10/10 cloud stretching over France, Belgium and Holland.

**1 December 1943**

Log Book – Spitfire IX – Fortress withdrawal cover, had to return, the boys went to Eindhoven. 120 aircraft raided many Forts bought it.

Allan Scott recalls:

With the Spitfire we could only provide short-range cover, and it proved inadequate when we started accompanying the heavy four-engine American bombers, the Flying Fortress or Liberators which might be returning, for example, from Berlin, Magdeburg or Brunswick. We could only escort them short distances into France or Holland and stay with them until they were safely over the English Channel. The American strategy was to fly the bombers in boxes to give maximum firepower from the combined gun turrets. On this occasion we picked up the first of the boxes of Forts returning from a raid over Eindhoven near the Zuider Zee. The state these aircraft were in was quite incredible. One with smoke pouring from one or two engines had a hole in the fuselage big enough to drive a car through. They had flown out on a beam. This was a radio signal sent out from Manston to help the Americans flying on instruments to get back from Germany, and would take them directly over Eindhoven. The Germans soon realised this and put heavy anti-aircraft guns directly under the beam, from which they were able to concentrate a cone of fire upwards. It devastated the bombers. The pilots' courage was beyond belief and unsurpassed – to see a box of aircraft ahead of them flying through this intense onslaught and to keep flying through it themselves was unbelievable. There was no deviation.

**12 December 1943**
Log Book – Spitfire IX – Fighter Sweep in support of Maurauders raiding Schipol, swept Amsterdam and Utrecht area, went in by Rotterdam. Bags of flak (and I can say that again). Two flamers, two Maurauders went into the drink.

**6 January 1944**
Log Book – Spitfire IX – Fighter umbrella to Mosquitos bombing construction works between Rouen and Dieppe. Swept Rouen area, we were bounced by about 30 Me 109s and FW 190s, had a bit of a scrap, hell of a shambles, bags of fun and games.

The construction works Johnnie referred to in his log book were in fact 'No-ball' targets, this the name given to targets against the German V1 or V2 rocket or weapon sites. The Mosquitos tried various techniques in attacking 'No-ball' sites. The normal method was to go low level all the way, but this had resulted in aircraft sustaining damage from 20mm flak near the coast. 'No-ball' targets were far too small to get four aircraft over within 11 seconds, which was the delay they had on the 500lb bombs, so they crossed the Channel at low level and then climbed as they reached the coast to about 3,000ft to avoid the flak. Then they would split into pairs for their targets and get down on the deck again. They would then run the gauntlet of further flak, given away by a distinctive red glow emanating from the woods below and arching rapidly towards them. Inevitably there were casualties. Lots of them.

**21 January 1944**
Log Book – Spitfire IX – Fighter Sweep in support of Bostons, Maurauders and Mitchells. ⚔ Went in at Cayeux. Swept Albert area. Approx 20 nice little yellow-nosed FW 190s. We met a Me 210 and I disintegrated it. A beautiful flamer after a 4 second squirt.

**24 January 1944**
Log Book – Spitfire IX – Withdrawal cover to Fortresses. Rendezvous Brussels. Went in just past Liege. Most god awful show yet. Bags of twitch. Landed at Manston with 6 gallons left. Got back by the grace of firkin. Paddy Goode killed and CO nearly was. The rest of us nearly too! What a day!!

By now Pete Wickham had been promoted from squadron leader to wing commander of 122 Wing 2nd TAF and was replaced by Squadron Leader Archie Stewart, who had come across from 65 Squadron, also part of 122 Wing. To overcome the Spitfire's short-range problem, the squadron soon changed from Spitfire IXs to American P-51 Mustangs. These had been fitted with the Merlin engine and long-range tanks which enabled them to fly for up to 5 hours, ideal for providing long-range cover to the American bombers. Some pilots were less than impressed with the change. They had grown to love the Spitfire and it was a love affair dear to their hearts, as Mejor stated:

The Spitfire was undeniably a beauty. She had graceful feminine curves but was also robust and provocative. With fascination I admired her from a distance and walked over to her with out-stretched arms and joy in my heart. I had longed for this moment ever since I had said goodbye to her sister back in Malta almost a year ago. I was divinely blissful and looked forward to a long and happy relationship with the girl of my dreams. It proved to be a short-term relationship. No sooner had I cast eyes on her then the powers that be intervened and took her away from me. These same powers tried to compensate and comfort me by offering me her cousin from America. She was not as beautiful, being more masculine with angular limbs and even a bit of a paunch, but she was also both dynamic and submissive and it was not long before I developed a great affection for her too.

The Spitfire, and in particular the Mk IX, was still the best in their eyes and the only aircraft most of them were interested in flying. On the morning the Gravesend Wing – as they had become known, composed of 19, 65 and 122 Squadrons – had the bombshell dropped that they were to have their Spitfires replaced by Mustangs, men stood there open-mouthed and in disbelief. This just could not be true. Mustangs, P-51s – American junk, they thought! To exchange their beloved Spitfires for such rubbish, had the Air Ministry gone off their rockers? This was intolerable. By the evening their anger had deteriorated to such an extent that it developed into a mass drunken brawl and resulted in fairly expensive repairs having to be carried out to the Mess!

After his first flight in the Mustang, Johnnie Mejor recorded, 'What beautiful aircraft Spitfires are!'

They need not have been so angry or worried. The original Mustang had been powered by an Allison engine and was fast and had good handling qualities, but above 15,000ft it proved useless as the engine had only a single stage compressor. A Rolls Royce test pilot had suggested fitting it with a Merlin engine, the same as the Spitfire IX, and this had flown for the first time back in 1942. The success of the match of the aircraft to the engine exceeded all expectations, so this much-modified fighter was born and became one of the best fighters of the war.

February 1944 was spent working up experience on the Mustangs, and then it was back on operations in March. Long-range escorts were still provided to American Fortresses and

Liberators bombing Germany. Allan Scott takes up his recollection of operations at the time:

> As it was such a long distance, the whole route was split into sections. If our squadron had the section which would actually fly over the target of Berlin, for instance, we would fly out to Berlin and join the bombers to give them air cover from German fighters until they were leaving. We would then start to fly back and the next squadron of Mustangs would take over as cover for that particular section, and so on.

It was frightening and sheer bloody physically exhausting. Sometimes they were in the air for over 3 or 4 hours if a return journey to a raid on Berlin was needed. For example:

**6 March 1944**
Log Book – Mustang III – Withdrawal cover to 640 Fortresses and Liberators – 3.35 hours Got as far as Neinburg, SE of Bremen. Escorted a lame Liberator back to England. Flak coming out of Amsterdam and the Dutch coast.

Unbeknown to Mejor at the time, this was the day the US 8th Air Force mounted its first full-scale daylight attack on Berlin. As a result of the hard-fought battles on the way to the target, over it and during their return flights, sixty-nine American bombers and eleven fighters failed to return. In no other day's fighting before or after this raid would the 8th Air Force lose more aircraft. One of the Mustang pilots succeeded in limping more than 250 miles across northern Germany with an engine running progressively rougher, but protected by his comrades:

> I kept going trying to get as far west as I could. Then just before the Dutch border, the engine began to get really hot and the

cockpit started to fill with smoke. I knew the time had come to bail out. As the engine died completely I released the canopy and followed the normal bail out drill: selecting full nose down trim, rolled the aircraft on to its back holding it straight and level, then released the stick and straps at the same time. The nose of the aircraft should have swung up sharply and I should have been thrown clear but because there was no power on, the nose of the aircraft immediately fell and I failed to clear the aircraft. I struggled back into the cockpit and turned the aircraft the right way up but in the process had lost quite a lot of height and the second time I tried to get out I was desperate. I just stood on the seat and kicked out and found myself falling clear. After a short fall I pulled my ripcord and as the chute popped I saw my aircraft hit the ground.

**8 March 1944**
Log Book – Mustang III – Withdrawal cover to 520 Fortresses and 190 Liberators bombing Berlin rail targets 4.25 hours. Picked up Forts 20 miles SE of Hamburg. Only six left in the Squadron. Went down on 2 Me 109s attacking Forts. My engine started smoking so I had to pull out. CO got shot at by Forts and had to break thus losing certain victory. Trigger happy Yanks! No other joy.

Allan Scott recalled:

Flying these long trips at 30,000ft for 3 or 4 hours or so in cramped cold and in an unpressurised cockpit was daunting and tiring, and certainly not as pleasant as flying the Spitfires, but at least we were able to give the fighter cover that had been so desperately needed.

As they were flying more and more over enemy territory there was concern for the pilots if they did have to bail out. Survival on the ground would be paramount. Scott again takes up the story:

It was decided that practice at survival would be a great asset. So the Intelligence Officers arranged a special exercise. Taking part, I joined up with Johnnie Mejor. He and I had become good friends, we looked after each other in the air and had often flown together as a pair and we looked after each other on the ground. We were transported to an unknown destination. Dressed as though we had 'baled' out, in blue pullovers, scarf and flying boots, we were dumped out of the truck and told to find our way back to the station at Gravesend. All road signs and names on railway stations had of course been taken down earlier in the war and the British countryside looked bleak. We could have been anywhere in Europe so the exercise was realistic.

We found ourselves in the middle of a field without a clue where we should go next. Our best plan of action, we concluded, would be to walk along the edge of the field in the hope of reaching a road. I had a button compass with me so on finding the road we decided to head north. We edged our way slowly along when suddenly out of nowhere men with rifles appeared. Someone, presumably a farmer, must have spotted us and immediately called the Home Guard. Our exercise in survival and avoiding capture had not lasted long and it was all I could do to surpass a wry grin. We did continue as ordered and that was to speak no English. After much gesturing we put our hands up and walked with the guards behind us, with their rifles at our backs. It was at this point that I began to get nervous. From what they were saying, it was obvious that they thought we were Germans and would have shot us had we tried anything. Johnnie, on the other hand, was thoroughly enjoying himself and entered the spirit of the exercise with full vigour and played the part of a 'German' very well. Too well in fact and this made me more nervous, and as he continued to play along his act was getting more risky.

We arrived at last at a police station and were locked in a cell. It was not long before an army Intelligence officer arrived to interrogate us.

Johnnie was by now in his element and kept up his part as the downed German and gave the Intelligence officer a rough time, picked up the daily newspaper and threw it down in disgust claiming it all to be lies, lies and propaganda. Bristling with rage and red in colour, the officer picked up the paper and departed. Alone, I told Johnnie that I thought it had gone far enough and that we should tell them we were on RAF exercise and produce our 1250 RAF ID cards. These were hidden in our flying boots. Johnnie was still reluctant to give in but did so eventually. What followed was even more uncomfortable. The surprise and anger on the face of the Intelligence officer was all too apparent and he was not best pleased and took a very dim view of the whole thing. Although the RAF has informed local areas of the exercise, this message had not filtered through to the little village of Green Street Green. After apologies all round, we were 'released' but the exercise had taught us how things could go wrong in occupied Europe and Johnnie's German could be saved for another day!

After the escapades of them trying to be Germans in England and avoiding capture, normal squadron life was resumed.

There seemed to be fewer daylight raids into Germany now and their escort role changed. More escorts were given to Beaufighters of the North Coates Strike Wing fitted with torpedoes attacking German shipping in the Frisian Islands.

By now Mejor had been awarded the Distinguished Flying Cross – this announced in the *London Gazette* on 14 April, 'Acting Flight Lieutenant John George MEJOR (119016), Royal Air Force Volunteer Reserve No 122 Squadron'. His citation read and described him as, 'A most aggressive and determined fighter pilot'.

### 20 April 1944
Log Book – Mustang III – Roadstead to Frisian Islands. Fighter cover to Beaus. 3 hours. Enemy convoy sighted off Heligoland

Bight. Saw one ship torpedoed and 3 pranged with cannon. Bags of heavy and light flak at us from ships and the coast. One Beau went in No one in dinghy.

Our task was to give them fighter cover over the target. The flak was fierce, not only from the ships but from guns based on the islands mostly aimed at the attacking Beaufighters but bursts would get through to us circling above. I did witness one of the Beaus taking a direct hit. It must have caught the torpedo because there was an almighty flash before it went into the sea. However the raid was successful as the convoy was completely destroyed and we escorted the remaining bombers back to base at a more reasonable height, remembering there is nothing more exhilarating than skimming over the waves at zero height to give the enemy no advance warning!

**26 April 1944**
Log Book – Mustang III – Roadstead to Heligoland Bight/Frisian Isles – Enemy convoy sighted and duly pranged. Bags of light flak from the Frisians.

**27 April 1944**
Log Book – Mustang III – Target support Maurauders bombing Arras and Cambrai – swept target area, some Huns came up but they would not let us go after them. Flak too accurate.

**29 April 1944**
Log Book – Mustang III – Escort Forts from North Hanover – some accurate flak, damaged.

**30 April 1944**
Log Book – Mustang III – Ranger aerodrome strafing – flak at deck level, hit in tail. Burst 100 feet beneath.

The few operational flights there were did not fill the pilots with
enthusiasm, as Allan Scott reported:

> We were sent on a few operational flights, but our role had changed,
> that is we escorted Beaufighters and Mosquitos in search of shipping
> along the enemy coast from Belgium to up to the northern tip of
> Jutland and Heligoland Bight. This meant flying at low altitudes, often
> in poor visibility, and it was not very exciting sitting in a single engine
> plane over the sea for up to 4 hours at a time, with little or no chance
> of being rescued should something go wrong. One was inclined to
> listen very closely to the engine on these flights and the wags declared
> that our ears grew noticeably larger during these operations!

By the end of April, further noticeable changes began to take
place in their operational deployment. Scott continued:

> A few more trips escorting the Forts in May but mostly we were
> now tasked with dive bombing targets in France for the build up to
> the D-Day invasion which we knew to be imminent, but of course
> had no idea where or when.

**2 May 1944**
Log Book – Mustang III – Dive bombing marshalling yards at
Mantes – Gassicourt – why does this bloody flak always go for me?
Once again hit in the prop!

Where and when the invasion was to take place was known only
to a handful of people. It was of course imperative to keep secret
exactly where the Allies intended to land, and much was done
to deceive and lead the Germans astray regarding this. These
measures proved so successful that for a long time Hitler insisted
that the landings in Normandy were mere deceptions and that the
main landings and invasion would take place further north in the

area of the Pas de Calais. Hitler had put much effort into fortifying every part of the European coastline where landings could possibly be made, and it was no secret that it had been dubbed 'Fortress Europe'. These fortifications would no doubt cause the invading forces untold losses so it was vital to weaken them as much as possible prior to any invasion. The Germans' lines of communication to the coastal areas would need to be crippled without giving the game away to where the invasion would be, but also to hamper the movement of enemy troops and reinforcements to the whole of the coast. Their role in the early stages was to escort the bombers doing these attacks, but because of the Mustang's range and carrying capacity, the decision was taken to form an independent offensive unit and they were renamed 122 Wing of the 2nd Tactical Air Force. In place of the drop tanks, two 500lb bombs were slung under the wings and they were dispatched to planned targets or to search for targets of opportunity.

### 6 May 1944
Log Book – Mustang III – to Predannack and then Ranger in search of Enemy Aircraft Bay of Biscay and Bordeaux Tours! Wizzo show. Strafing camps and Hun army trucks. Good burst at a Ju 34 on ground south of Poitiers. Hit in tail by flak. Scotty hit too. Scotty strafed a French concentration camp north of Bayonne.

### 10 May 1944
Log Book – Mustang III – Fort withdrawal in Brunswick area – flak, prepared to bale out over Holland.

Allan Scott reported:

Still now and again an escort operation for the Forts and Liberators, especially on a target where they needed fighter cover. On one occasion this was Brunswick. Unfortunately when we reached the position where we would pick them up, levels of cloud were obscuring the whole area and we were unable to find them. The CO decided that we should split into pairs, climb through the cloud and report the height of any layers of clearance that the Forts would be flying in, and the squadron could climb to and reformate. Not being good at instrument flying I closed on Johnnie Mejor and we entered cloud at around 5,000ft. I had one hell of a time staying with him and we didn't break cloud until 34,000ft. I sweated all the way up that ascent until I was hugely relieved to see the sun at last. Of course at this height the Forts would certainly not be flying, which meant that we had to make an even more nerve-wracking descent. I cannot describe the task I had given myself to close format on another aircraft in thick cloud. It was as terrifying as dogfighting with an Me 109 on your tail. Through it all came the incessant cold, salty sweat running down the face and into your mouth. We broke cloud cover over the Zuider Zee and I was so relieved to see the deck again I almost choked. We were greeted with flak which seemed a cruel welcome after what we had been through. Johnnie said he had been hit and would have to bale out. I flew round him but could see no damage. I managed to calm him down and as we were so close to the sea, to persuade him to head back to Manston. We were not out of trouble yet. There was always the anxious look out for Me 109s. Had they been around we would have ended up in a dogfight which did not appeal to either of us but we managed to creep out and belt back to the good old white cliffs of Dover as fast as we could. This was an experience I never wanted to repeat but it was probably a most effective lesson. It made me all the more determined to become more proficient at instrument flying.

**11 May 1944**
Log Book – Mustang III – Dive bombing marshalling yards at Charleroi – bags of flak over target and on the way out. Mejor is hit once again. Bombing good strafed gunners.

These attacks, carrying two 500lb bombs attached under the wings of the Mustangs, ran almost constantly each day, right through into June. The pilots were shattered. At the beginning of the month the aircraft had broad black and white Allied Expeditionary Air Force identity stripes painted around the wings and fuselage. D-Day loomed.

**6 June 1944**
Log Book – Mustang III – Beach Head

Mejor reported:

> It was still dark and heavy blasts of wind shook our aircraft and the rain pounded on them as we sat in our cockpits and waited for the green flare that would be the signal for the start of our engines. We had drunk our early morning cup of tea in a chilly mess tent and in the operations room we had been able to study the invasion area marked with crayon on a large wall map. The landing beaches had been given names such as Utah, Omaha, Gold, Juno and Sword. We had listened to Spy's report on the weather for the past 24 hours and knew the decision had been taken to go. This was it.

It was expected that fighting on the beaches would be ferocious but it would be the wing's task to search out the German supply routes to the bridgehead and do all they could to delay German reinforcements. Mejor continued:

> There was only a faint hint of grey light in the eastern sky when the flare went up and cast a glow on the base of the low-lying clouds and rivulets of rain on the canopy over our heads. The Met officer had said that even though the wind was less severe on the other side of the Channel, the area of rain stretched inland from the beaches and we could expect drizzle and poor visibility. Now our

engines were started and in the growing light we taxied into position for take-off. Engines full power, throttles open and away. Wing set course due south. The blanket of cloud lay depressingly low over the sea and the drizzle greatly reduced our vision. We passed many ships in the Channel, sailing south, but it was not until after about 15 minutes flying that we entered the Baie de la Seine and caught sight of the main invasion fleet. In spite of our low altitude and poor visibility limiting our radius of view, we could see literally hundreds of ships in the Baie. In the choppy sea landing craft were darting between the large transport ships and shore, and further out to sea, flashes from the larger warships' guns were visible through the murkiness. Fires were scattered along the beaches and the smoke from them blended with the drizzle and low cloud and did nothing to improve the visibility. Now Wing Commander's voice over the RT – 'All right chaps we'd better split up here. The visibility is too poor for a Wing formations. Each squadron to carry on independently. Good luck.'

Onwards we flew at 500ft and [as] we passed the coast traces of flak rose to meet us but in a short time we were clear of the coastal defences. Our hopes that inland there would be better visibility and cloud conditions did not materialise and we roamed around at low altitude but did not see much. At one point we met a bunch of Spitfires at the same height and it was only by the grace of god we averted any collisions. The incident was sufficiently unnerving to convince the CO that flying around treetop height in murky conditions in close proximity to other groups of friendly aircraft, even with black and white invasion stripes, was not a good idea so he set course for home and ordered a return to base.

And that was it for Johnnie Mejor and Allan Scott. Both were shattered. They had been allowed one last operational flight due to the importance of D-Day but they were both operationally tour-expired and were posted on leave the very next day.

Mejor's log book was signed off by his Wing Commander Flying – G.R. 'Robin' Johnston – as above the average as a fighter pilot, 122 Wing 2nd TAF 07/06/1944, and by the Officer Commanding 122 Wing, Wing Commander 'Bunny' Currant. Both wished him good luck.

# Epilogue

David Macfarlane could not sail back with the remaining crew from Malta in the *Melbourne Star* because of his illness. She sailed again, this time on 22 March 1943 from Liverpool on her way to Sydney through the Panama Canal. She carried seventy-seven crew, eleven gunners and thirty-one passengers, and was commanded by Captain James Bennett Hall. Among the crew on board the *Melbourne Star* were those who had been in her during her historic voyage to Malta in August 1942, under Mac's command. The ship carried a heavy cargo of torpedoes, ammunition and other munitions of war, and once clear of the most dangerous submarine area sailed unescorted.

We know few of the details of her loss, except that at about 3 a.m. on Friday 2 April 1943, when 480 miles south-east of Bermuda (28° 5'N 57° 30'W) in bad weather that was raging all over the North Atlantic, she was struck by two torpedoes almost simultaneously. The double explosion detonated portions of her dangerous cargo, for three-quarters of the vessel was destroyed in a flash. The explosions were so sudden and devastating that neither passengers nor crew could muster at their boat stations, even if any boats had been left intact. Practically the entire complement perished simultaneously and the shattered remains of the ship went to the bottom in less than 2 minutes. As she foundered, several of the life-saving rafts floated free, to which a few of the survivors managed to scramble. Their plight was made even worse by the heavy sea and low visibility, and when the dawn came only eleven people were left alive on two rafts. She had been torpedoed by *U-129*. Only four survivors were picked up thirty-nine days later in a Catalina flying boat that took them back to Bermuda.

Macfarlane had not been with her when she was lost, and the next three years saw several appointments, but nothing of the magnitude of Operation Pedestal and these were largely uneventful. Two years after the war ended he began a long and unbroken connection with the London South America service.

Initially appointed to the *Argentina Star*, he was transferred to the *Paraguay Star* in 1950 and, apart from a short break in 1957 when he commanded the *Adelaide Star* to New Zealand, he remained in charge of the *Paraguay Star* until his retirement in 1961. His love of gardening and golf remained but sadly he died on 16 October 1984, aged 89.

By a strange quirk of fate, Johnnie Mejor and Allan Scott were both posted to 39 Maintenance Unit (MU) at RAF Colerne just outside Bath as test pilots. This was a great experience for both of them. Test flying from the MUs was vital in getting the aircraft up to standard and ensuring they were safe before being sent to operational squadrons. It gave Mejor the opportunity to fly all sorts of different aircraft including the Spitfire again, but also the Seafire, Anson, Oxford, Master and even the veritable old Blenheim. Mejor and Scott both had a few near misses in aircraft that refused to do what they wanted them to do, but it was largely an enjoyable and stress-free time for them both. The nearest Mejor came to any sort of trouble was in a forced landing in a Master in December 1944, and his only comment was, 'force landed base wheels down, engine cut out 4,000ft!'

By now Mejor had met Cecile, who would later become his wife. He had been introduced by his friend Derek Clarke, who had invited her to a ball at RAF Colerne. Their first meeting did not go to plan and Cecile was less than impressed, 'He shook hands with me and then went off and danced with someone else!' She had grown up in Clifton in Bristol, and was PA to Sir S. George White of the Bristol Aeroplane Company (BAC) based at Filton, Bristol. He was the grandson of the founder of the company and had been educated himself at Harrow school and Cambridge. He had become a director of the company in 1942 and ultimately would serve as director and deputy chairman. Sir George was, Cecile remembered, a bit of a visionary and in planning for post-war manufacturing of BAC encouraged the production of the Bristol

Freighter and quality motor cars, but was responsible for the direction of the aircraft and armament divisions of BAC during the war and the link between the Ministry of Aircraft production and the company. He was held in the highest regard.

Mejor decided that a charm offensive was needed to impress Cecile so phoned her whilst she was at her work and told her to go up on the roof of the building at Filton at midday on the dot. Sure enough she did, more out of curiosity than anything else, but right on cue, Mejor flashed by in his Spitfire, beat up the airfield, waggled his wings and was away again. She did not wave, for fear of getting him into trouble. This may well have worked, except that she had been followed up onto the roof by one Sir S. George White, who was less than impressed with the Spitfire flyboy! She need not have worried about getting Mejor into trouble – his Spitfire had no markings. It was from the Maintenance Unit so could not be traced!

Maybe the charm offensive worked because he and Cecile were married on 1 August 1945 in Clifton, with Allan Scott as Mejor's best man. It seemed only right that he should be. They had looked after each other when they first met in Malta, been posted to the same 122 Squadron when back on operations and also to the same MU at Colerne. They had become great friends and were a good foil for each other. A telegram from family unable to make the wedding read, 'F/Lt and Mrs C. Mejor, 11 Royal York Crescent, Clifton, Bristol – Congratulations to you both on your complete victory. Delighted that all organised resistance has come to an end! Love Ian and Eileen Mejor.'

Mejor decided to stay in the RAF and in 1945 was offered a permanent commission and became a regular officer. A couple of administrative posts followed until 1949, when he opened a new phase in his life by attending an Intelligence course and was appointed Group Intelligence Officer at HQ 46 Group. He was then posted overseas to Ottawa and Strategic Intelligence with the

John and Cecile's engagement, August 1944. Allan Scott and Dessie Hair are to the far right. (J.G. Mejor)

John and Cecile married in 1945. (J.G. Mejor)

Royal Canadian Air Force, where he helped to assess the capabilities of the Soviet and Chinese Air Forces for the RCAF as the very real threat of the Cold War developed, and in the light of the Korean War experience.

Mejor was finally given command of his own squadron as CO of 130 (Punjab) Squadron, successfully flying Vampire Mk Vs, North American Sabre Mk IVs and finally Hunter Mk IVs. From their base in Bruggen, Germany, they operated in what was described as peacetime. The reality was somewhat different. For the RAF the threat was very real and the squadron endured long periods of almost daily high alerts, flying and confronting aggressive attempts by Soviet MIG fighters over German air space as they continued to probe their capabilities and air defences.

After he was posted from 130 (Punjab) Squadron back to England he worked on attachment from the RAF at the Air Ministry in London, until the time of defence cuts loomed and led the RAF to reduce its wage bill by capping promotion. Among the first group to go were foreign-born officers, including Johnnie Mejor. Had it not been for this decision, Mejor would have remained with the RAF for the rest of his career, but he left the RAF in 1964 and moved to Exmouth.

The romantic in him had not been lost; he presented Cecile with a rose from the overgrown garden of a house in Exmouth overlooking the bay and told her that one day it would be her garden. The formalities were soon completed and they moved to Maer Craig. Their two daughters, Jane and Sally, arrived and they remained in the same house for the rest of their lives. It is a wonderfully quiet place. Mejor finished his working career with Devon County Council and became chairman of the Devon Conservation Forum, being responsible for the preservation of a number of fine historical buildings when conservation was not fashionable and there was a lack of funding. His passion for conservation shone through to such an extent that he set up the annual John Mejor Award for practical conservation work and promotion of the beauty of the countryside in Devon, the United Kingdom and internationally.

Sadly, in later life he developed dementia and required care, and Johnnie Mejor died on 24 March 2010, aged 88.

# Bibliography & Sources

Barnham, Denis, *One Man's Window* (William Kimber 1956)

Crabb, Brian, *Operation Pedestal* (Butler Tanner 2014)

Douglas Hamilton, James, *The Air Battle for Malta* (Airlife Publishing 1981)

Hill, Roger, *Destroyer Captain* (Granada Publishing 1979)

HMSO, *Merchantmen at War* (HMSO 1944)

Houlton, Johnnie, *Spitfire Strikes* (John Murray 1985)

Jackson, Bill, *Air Sea Rescue during the Siege of Malta* (Matador 2010)

Mansfield, Angus, *Barney Barnfather* (The History Press 2008)

Moses, Sam, *At All Costs* (Random House 2007)

Rae, Jack, *Kiwi Spitfire Ace* (Grub Street 2001)

Rolls, William, *Spitfire Attack* (William Kimber 1987)

Scott, Allan, *Born to Survive* (Ellingham Press, 2013)

Shankland, Peter and Hunter, Anthony, *Malta Convoy* (Collins 1961)

Shores, Christopher, *2nd TAF* (Osprey 1970)

Shores, Christopher and Cull, Brian, *Malta: The Spitfire Year* (Grub Street 1991)

Smith, Peter, *Pedestal* (William Kimber 1970)
Smith, Peter, *Eagles War* (Crecy Publishing Ltd 1995)
Wellum, Geoffrey, *First Light* (Penguin 2002)

# Index

If you enjoyed this book, you may also be interested in…

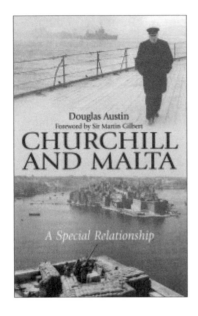

## Churchill and Malta

DOUGLAS AUSTIN

978 0 7509 6069 4

This is the compelling story of the special relationship between Winston Churchill and the people of Malta. During six visits over a period of forty years he came to understand and support the aspirations of the Maltese people and in the Second World War the bonds linking them were tempered in fire and destruction. In those dark days Churchill's determination to defend the island and his faith in the courage of the Maltese people never wavered.